It's News To Me!

Messages Of Hope For Those Who Haven't Heard

Gospel Sermons For Advent/Christmas/Epiphany

Cycle A

Linda Schiphorst McCoy

CSS Publishing Company, Inc., Lima, Ohio

IT'S NEWS TO ME!
MESSAGES OF HOPE FOR THOSE WHO HAVEN'T HEARD

Copyright © 2001 by
CSS Publishing Company, Inc.
Lima, Ohio

Library of Congress Cataloging-in-Publication Data

McCoy, Linda Schiphorst, 1945-
   It's news to me! : messages of hope for those who haven't heard : Gospel sermons for Advent, Christmas, and Epiphany, cycle A / Linda Schiphorst McCoy.
      p. cm.
   ISBN 0-7880-1822-1 (alk. paper)
   1. Advent sermons. 2. Christmas sermons. 3. Epiphany season—Sermons. 4. Bible. N.T. Gospels—Sermons. 5. Sermons, American—21st century. I. Title.
BV4254.5 .M33 2001
252'.61—dc21   2001025073
                                                                                                                    CIP

For more information about CSS Publishing Company resources, visit our website at www.csspub.com.

ISBN 0-7880-1822-1   PRINTED IN U.S.A.

I dedicate this collection of messages to my husband Mike and our daughter Erin, who have always been on the path with me as encourager, advocate, critic, and supporter. I love you both.

It is dedicated with great love and admiration to those who are in ministry with me at **THE GARDEN**, *A Blossom of St. Luke's United Methodist Church.*

Thanks to those who have taken the time to read and give feedback on these messages, offering comments, constructive criticism, and helpful insights: Mike McCoy, Mary Benedict, and Parry Tillett.

A special thank you to my longtime colleague and former senior pastor of St. Luke's United Methodist Church, Dr. E. Carver McGriff, one of those who has always encouraged me in my ministry, and who got me into writing this book.

In addition, I must say a special word of thanks to P. Wayne Trevathan, who believed in me and my possibilities in ministry long before I believed in myself. I must express my deep appreciation of and value for all the colleagues with whom I have been privileged to serve at St. Luke's. Without your example of constantly striving for excellence, and trying to be faithful to God, I would not be the person I am today.

I thank you all.

Table Of Contents

Introduction

The sermons you are about to read have been preached in their entirety or in part at THE GARDEN, *A Blossom of St. Luke's United Methodist Church,* in Indianapolis, Indiana. THE GARDEN, a true "God Thing," has been the ministry of which I've been a part since 1995. Meeting at a dinner theater, THE GARDEN attempts to reach out to share the unconditional love of God with those who have never heard or truly experienced it.

It is probably important to understand the context for which the messages were prepared. THE GARDEN is a gathering of people who have either never been a part of a traditional congregation, or have found themselves "turned off" or "turned out" by the church. And yet they are hungry, hungry for a word of hope, hungry for a sense of acceptance, hungry for a touch of love, and many of them claim to have found that at THE GARDEN.

Our services are short (due to the time constraints of the theater in which we're housed), and to the point. Every song, every video clip, every drama sketch, everything we do and say must carry the message and theme for that particular Sunday. The service is very highly integrated, and everything must fit together to communicate the message we are trying to convey.

It's important to us that we share a message that is relevant, that connects with those who are there with us, and a message that leaves them with something to carry home for the week ahead. Because we consider worship a time for celebration and inspiration, we attempt to be positive, encouraging, while striving to touch a chord deep inside. We do not try to instruct or teach in this setting, but leave that to our small group experiences.

Typically, the heart of the message is twelve minutes long, with a closing word that is anywhere from thirty seconds to two minutes. The sermons assume that those who are participating in our worship time have little or no prior experience in the faith.

The versions of the Bible which are used at THE GARDEN vary, and that is reflected in the translations and paraphrases that I have cited in this book. Usually we use those that seem most easily understood, either *Today's English Version, The Message,* or the *Contemporary English Version.*

Clearly, the Gospel passages that are assigned are rich with subject matter for preaching, and there are many directions in which the speaker could go. However, I have chosen only the one — usually the most obvious — which could most directly relate to the needs of the people to whom the sermon is addressed.

I would urge the pastors who are reading this collection of sermons to look at them for the germination of ideas for your own messages. I know that I cannot re-preach one of my own sermons, and can't imagine trying to preach something that someone else has prepared! I hope, however, you will find stories and resources that can be of assistance in that never-ending challenge of preparing a message to share in worship that touches hearts and changes lives. Godspeed in your journey.

I hope that you, the reader, will find these messages helpful and meaningful, for I believe God's word of hope, faith, and love is the most important word we can ever hear or share. If we don't share the Good News in ways that people can hear and understand, they will miss the most vital word of life that exists.

May God bless our mutual ministry together.

When We Don't Know

Just a few days before writing this message, I conducted a memorial service for a 60-year-old man who was the picture of health until three months before his death. He was active, vibrant, only recently retired, and looking forward to years of good life with his wife and family and friends. Nonetheless, pancreatic cancer had done its work, and quickly, and he was gone. It was the general consensus that it was too soon for his life to end; he was too young to die.

That experience came to mind as I was reading and studying the Bible passage for today. Scholars are not in total agreement about what it means, and no one knows for sure the point Jesus intended to make. One thing we need to understand is that the people who lived at that time expected Jesus to come back, and put everything right. In their minds, his return could happen at any time.

Clearly, that did not happen, and we're left wondering exactly what the point of this Bible passage is. I know there are those who await what is commonly referred to as "The Second Coming," but that's not where I am. While I admit to being as much in the dark as anyone else about this, I really believe that Jesus is setting forth a very existential question about life. It has to do with being ready for our lives to come to an end, whenever that may be.

As I read and reread the passage, it seemed to be asking the eternal, existentialist question: "If my life were to end today, is it the way I'd want it to be? If I were to die in my sleep tonight, would everything end the way I wanted it to? If I leave home tomorrow for work, and don't return in the evening, is my life story the one I want told?"

The Bible passage seems to be challenging us to get our lives together, because we don't know which day will be our last on this earth. Joan Baez was really saying the same thing when she commented, "You don't get to choose how you're going to die. Or when. You can only decide how you're going to live. Now."[1] That's the choice each one of us makes every minute of every day: how we're going to live in this moment. As Annie Dillard said in *The Writing Life,* "How we spend our days is, of course, how we spend our lives."[2]

It's interesting to reflect on this question, given some of the events of the last year of the century. In April of 1999, two students opened fire at Columbine High School in Littleton, Colorado, killing twelve other students and one faculty member before taking their own lives. In the time that has elapsed since the massacre, we've heard story after story of students who claimed their faith in God, even knowing it would spell certain death.

We've heard many stories about the kind of person each one was, and the kind of lives they lived. They were young people who expected to live long, full lives, but that was not to be the case. They didn't know when it would end, and that day came in an unexpected and horrifying way.

In the summer of 1999, the entire nation watched and waited for news of the fate of John F. Kennedy, Jr., his wife Caroline, and her sister. Their small plane vanished as they were approaching the airport in Hyannis Port, Massachusetts. Finally, after a massive search, the wreckage of the plane was found at the bottom of the sea, and their families and friends began their all-too-common plight of mourning the dead.

It was interesting, in the midst of all the media hype, to hear about how these well-known people had lived. We heard about their last day on this earth, and from all we saw and read, they were good people. Friends and acquaintances alike talked about how John Jr. tried to live his life in ways that were as normal as the lives you and I try to live. Once again, these events reminded me that we may be living our last day on earth right now, and we are

10

making our legacy right this very minute. We make our mark with everything we say, and everything we do.

In some ways, it may be like something that can happen to any of us, and did happen in my life. My father lived alone in the home he and my mother bought in 1932. She had died six years earlier, and he managed quite well until that last unexpected illness. One day he was doing okay and the next he was on his way by ambulance to Indianapolis to undergo the first surgery of his life. The trauma was too much for him, and he died two weeks later.

When we went to his home the day after his death, we could see the traces of the life he had lived. We could see in the garage, his favorite place, what he had been doing and what he intended to do by the tools that were there. A look in the refrigerator told us what he'd last had for dinner, and the freezer revealed what was next on the agenda. Talking to a neighbor told us how recently the lawn had been mowed. Everywhere we looked there was evidence of the life he had lived and the person he was.

The same thing is true for all of us. The reality is that each of us leaves a trail behind us as proof of our having been here. As a result, it's probably important to think about the kind of tracks we're leaving behind. What will be said about us when it's all over? How will we be remembered?

Sometimes we can tell the legacy that's been left behind by wandering through a cemetery and reading all the inscriptions we find on tombstones. I haven't done that for a long time, but the other day, I happened to download some epitaphs from e-mail. Listen to some of them, and see what they tell us about the person who died.

There's this one in Silver City, Nevada. It reads: "Here lays Butch, we planted him raw. He was quick on the trigger, but slow on the draw." You may have heard about this one from a Georgia cemetery. It reads, "I told you I was sick!" In Thurmont, Maryland, we find this one: "Here lies an atheist, all dressed up and no place to go." Or this one from somewhere in England: "Dead at 30; buried at 60." Those tombstones tell us a lot about the lives that were led and the legacies that were left.

Given all that, it's important to ask ourselves the questions: "How do we live to ensure the kind of legacy we want to leave behind? What is the better way to live?" For me, it has everything to do with living under the influence of God, and basing our lives on our faith in God. When we do that, the probability is that our lives will be different and more positive and fulfilling than if we choose another basis on which to live. When we're under God's influence, we begin to reflect a little of God's love and patience and kindness and goodness.

I believe faith in God causes us to *want* to live our lives differently. It's not that we're ordered or commanded to do that, but when our heart changes, so do our thoughts, words, and deeds. We make plenty of mistakes, and we wander off the path from time to time, but when we keep striving to be more loving in everything we say and do, we are leaving a positive legacy behind us.

It seems to me that there are two obvious marks of a life that is based on faith in God: kindness and love. As Isaac Bashevis Singer noted, "Kindness, I've discovered, is everything in life."[3] Kenneth Clark put it this way: "Ask any decent person what he thinks matters most in human conduct: five to one his answer will be 'kindness.' "[4]

The kind of thing I'm talking about is how we treat the person on the other end of the phone, or the clerk at the checkout lane in the grocery. It's how we treat friends and strangers alike. It's a gentle word; it's a warm smile; it's a bit more patience. Kindness is a more gentle way of living life.

The second mark of a life that is under God's influence is love. Some of you may be familiar with the name of Morrie Schwartz. Morrie was a professor at Brandeis University who had ALS, Lou Gehrig's Disease, and died a few years ago. However, in the process of his dying, he shared his wisdom and insights about life and death, about living and dying, that were captured in a book — *Tuesdays With Morrie* — written by one of his former students, Mitch Albom, a sportswriter for the Detroit *Free Press*. Morrie was also featured several times on *Nightline* with Ted Koppel, and his teachings touched millions of people.

On one of their regular Tuesday meetings, Morrie told Mitch that someone had asked him an interesting question the day before. The question was if he worried about being forgotten after he died. "Do you?" Mitch asked him. Morrie said he didn't think so, because he had so many people who had been involved with him in such close, intimate ways. And then he said, "Love is how you stay alive, even after you are gone."[5] Morrie knew what counts. He understood that love lasts forever.

I think he's right. There's only one thing that truly outlasts us, and lives forever, and that's love. When the body ceases to exist, one thing goes on — the love we have for our God and for our brothers and sisters everywhere. That love outlives us, and stays in the lives of those we have touched. Love is the best legacy we can leave. If we live our lives in love — for ourselves, for one another, for our God — then we are leaving a legacy that is truly eternal.

We never know which day will be our last on this earth. Perhaps it's a good idea to think about the kind of lives we're living. What are we leaving behind? What will our legacy be? Will it be a legacy of love and kindness?

Closing Word

Henry Ward Beecher once wrote: "We should so live and labor in our time that what came to us as seed may go to the next generation as blossom, and what came to us as blossom may go to them as fruit."[6]

As you leave here this morning, I hope and pray that the seeds and blossoms we pass along will be rooted in and filled with love. And go in peace. Amen.

---

1. Joan Baez, *Quotable Quotes* (Pleasantville, New York: Reader's Digest, 1997), p. 146.

2. Annie Dillard, *The Writing Life, Quotable Quotes* (Pleasantville, New York: Reader's Digest, 1997), p. 150.

3. Isaac Bashevis Singer, *Quotable Quotes* (Pleasantville, New York: Reader's Digest, 1997), p. 78.

4. Kenneth Clark, *Quotable Quotes* (Pleasantville, New York: Reader's Digest, 1997), p. 78.

5. Mitch Albom, *Tuesdays With Morrie* (New York: Doubleday, 1997), p. 133.

6. Henry Ward Beecher, source unknown.

Prepare For Arrival

Have you ever been on a plane and heard the captain tell the cabin crew to "prepare for arrival"? That announcement lets everyone know that the plane is approaching the gate, and the doors are about to open. When the passengers hear it, they immediately start to gather their belongings, put on coats, and prepare to de-plane.

That's like almost everything else in life. Virtually anything we do requires some sort of preparation and getting ready. On a plane we have to prepare the doors and the cabin for take-off and arrival. In school, we have to prepare our homework. We have to study in preparation for final exams, and we have to prepare the house and the meal before guests arrive. If we happen to be expecting a baby, we have to prepare the nursery, as well as preparing ourselves mentally, physically, and emotionally for what's about to happen. At this time of year, we have to make all our preparations in order to be ready for Christmas.

However, the reality is that we are not always ready when Christmas or any other major event happens in our lives. That was the case with us when our daughter Erin arrived. Erin is adopted, so her arrival was a bit more difficult to predict. We had been through all the infertility studies, and had decided to pursue the adoption route. However, this was at a time when it was becoming increasingly difficult to adopt, and the waiting lists were three or more years long! We made all the necessary contacts, and then began the task of waiting for the event to happen. Because it seemed so far away, we didn't even think about doing any preparations for

15

fear we'd be disappointed. Instead, I kept on teaching (my first career), and we began planning our next trip.

A few months later, just four days after Christmas vacation, at the end of a very long day of school, I was told that I had a phone call, and that my husband Mike had called and was on his way to the school. That seemed strange to me, because I knew he had just gone into a three-day planning session at his company. As soon as I got downstairs, picked up the phone, and heard the name of the caller, I knew what was going on. In disbelief, I heard the words, "We have a baby daughter for you. She was born yesterday, is very healthy, and she can be in your arms tomorrow. All you have to do is say, 'Yes,' and oh — by the way, you need to have a name for her."

Those next 24 hours were a whirlwind! We called our families; we called friends who had adopted a child just three months before for recommendations for a pediatrician, and for ideas about what we needed to get. They said, "Meet us at Ayr-way"— our forerunner of Target — "in thirty minutes," which we did, and then watched in amazement as they filled our shopping cart and steered us to the check-out lane.

Within 24 hours and 30 minutes of that original phone call, we had our beautiful daughter, Erin, in our arms. However, we were ill prepared to be parents! When we finally made our way home, we didn't have anywhere to put this precious child. I had called a friend who'd had a baby a year or so earlier, and she offered a cradle that would work for a while. But when we first walked in the door, there we were — the three of us — and very little else. After a few minutes, the doorbell started to ring and a baby cradle and baby things began to arrive, along with friends who turned out to be a big help! I had no idea how to make formula, so somebody was in the kitchen doing that, and others were helping get things set up in the little room upstairs where Erin was to sleep.

As you can imagine, we were totally exhausted by the time that day was over, and we collapsed and slept soundly — it never occurring to us that babies wake up in the night and want something to eat! Thank goodness our friends from Chicago had arrived and were spending the night, because Carol heard Erin crying, fed her, changed her, and put her back to bed, and we never heard a thing! It's a miracle she's made it to adulthood and the gracious young woman she is, because she certainly has had a set of parents who were poorly prepared for the task!

Our experience certainly flies in the face of the Bible passage for this morning which is talking about preparing and getting ready. In this passage, John the Baptist is paving the way for Jesus. He got people's attention and tried to prepare them for the arrival of the Savior. He's telling the people of that day and ours to "prepare the way for the Lord." In telling his listeners to prepare the way and make the path straight, he was echoing the words of the prophet Isaiah whom we read about in the Hebrew writings. He was making a reference to something people of the time would have understood.

The message as it came from Isaiah was to remind people of the necessity of preparing the roads for the coming of a king or ruler who would lead them. I guess in some ways the preparation needed for the arrival of a king then would be like a city getting ready for the arrival of the President today. Every detail of the President's itinerary is carefully crafted to make sure everything goes as smoothly and as safely as possible.

There were a couple of things the people of John the Baptist's time needed to do to get ready for the leader's arrival. They were to prepare the roads by clearing them of obstacles like boulders or stones that were in the way, and they were to smooth out all the bumps and dips that made the ride so rough and bumpy.

We can probably get a good idea of what those roads might have been like if we just think back to what happens around here in the early spring. After the cold and snow of winter, our streets are a mess with potholes and broken pavement everywhere. Our worst roads probably would seem like floating on a cloud compared to the roads of that day! The roads were terrible, and travel was rugged. To be asked to prepare the way for the king meant making the path smooth and less blocked and cluttered with obstacles.

In the same way that John the Baptist called on the people of his time to do whatever they needed to do to prepare for the arrival of the one they had been waiting for, he is doing the same thing for each of us even today. John the Baptist would urge us to do whatever we need to do to prepare for the arrival of the one we've been hearing about and looking for — the one who promises to change life as we know it.

We're encouraged to get ready for his coming, but even so, I would guess that most of us aren't there. We're simply not ready. The truth is that just in the same way that Erin surprised us by coming when we least expected, so it is with God. God's blessings often come to us in unexpected ways, at unexpected times, and in unexpected places, and it's easy to miss out if we're not ready. How is it possible to be totally prepared? What if we don't think we're really ready for the unexpected, for the surprising, for the wonderful things that God brings to our lives?

I'd like to suggest a couple of things we can do to get ready for Christmas this year, and they have nothing to do with trimming the tree. They're very basic, and the first has to do with being willing to say, "Yes," to whatever new and surprising comes into our lives. I hate to think what our lives would have been like had I said to that caller on that Thursday in January of 1975, "Oh, we can't ... after all we don't have the nursery ready, and we have a trip planned."

I'm so glad we said, "Yes," and I've learned a lesson from that. You and I may never feel ready enough, or good enough, or worthy enough for anything as overwhelming as God's unconditional love, but that's not the way God sees it. God offers it anyway, and we just have to say, "Yes," and accept it. It's a gift, freely given, and it's for you and for me. Being ready for Christmas really is about being ready to say, "Yes," and accept the surprises that come to us during this Christmas season.

There's a second thing I'd like to suggest when it comes to trying to prepare for Christmas, and that's the necessity of learning to slow down and stop and look and listen. It's a matter of being open and ready to see what is in front of us. Sometimes we just need to take a deep breath in the midst of all the hustle and bustle, and relax and let God in.

Maybe when we're in the middle of the mall, totally overwhelmed with a long shopping list and crowded stores, that just might be the moment we need to take a time-out. Perhaps we could get a cup of coffee and just sit down and observe the people around us. Maybe we could actually listen to the Christmas carols playing through the sound system, and remember what it's all about.

Sometimes God breaks through to us in some unexpected and surprising ways, and we just need to be open to receive. That happened to me during Erin's very first Christmas. It was Christmas Eve morning, and I had been out running some errands. As I was on my way home, I had the radio on in the car, and the station I was listening to was playing Christmas carols.

I was really only half-listening to the songs, but suddenly I became aware that "Silent Night" was playing, and I began singing along. Before I realized what was happening, I was overcome with emotion, and the tears began running down my cheeks. I was so taken with the words of that carol that I had to pull my car off the road until I could recover. I wasn't sure what was going on, and it wasn't until much later that I began to realize what had happened. God had broken through to me, and the truth of the Christmas message became real in a way it had never been before. In those moments, I experienced God's breaking into my little world in a surprising and beautiful way.

The truth is that you and I may never feel we're totally ready for Christmas, but our preparations really have nothing to do with the shopping and the wrapping and the decorating. Getting ready for Christmas is really about slowing down and preparing our hearts to say, "Yes," to God's incredible love.

Closing Word

My husband has a habit that I'm trying to acquire. When we fly into a different time zone, he always sets his watch to the time at our destination. That helps us start living in that time zone. I really think that's the way it is when it comes to Christmas. Maybe we need to set our clock to Christmas Time, and be prepared to live in this wondrous moment.

As you leave here this morning, know that the love of Christmas is all around us. Live in the midst of it; be prepared to receive it, and go in peace. Amen.

Advent 3
Matthew 11:2-11

Expecting

When a woman is pregnant, we often say she is "expecting." That is a good term for it, because she's expecting or anticipating that a baby will be born at some appointed time in the future, and along with that baby will come a whole wealth of other expectations. There will be expectations about who the baby will look like, and what that baby will be like. There will be expectations about the baby's future — the kind of life he or she will live; the kind of person the child will become. As V. S. Naipaul once said, "One isn't born one's self. One is born with a mass of expectations, a mass of other people's ideas — and you have to work through it all."[1]

How true that is! Expectations do play a major role in our lives. Even if we're just doing something as ordinary as driving down the road, we have expectations. We expect the other drivers to obey the traffic laws, and remain on their side of the highway, and we expect the same of ourselves. If we're gardeners, and plant some seeds, we have expectations. We expect those seeds to take root and grow and produce.

The same thing is true in many other situations as well. There are expectations of the kind of grades we'll get in school, or how we'll do in athletic endeavors. A teacher in the classroom has expectations of how students will learn and behave, and students have their expectations of what will happen in the class. The same is true in the workplace. Both employers and workers have their expectations of the work to be done, and what it takes to succeed. Anytime we're in a relationship with another person, most of us have some expectations of what that relationship should be, and the needs that are to be met as a part of that connection.

The issue of expectations does create a bit of a quandary. There are times when holding high expectations is a good thing. Having high expectations can often help us reach beyond what we thought possible. However, expectations can be tricky, and sometimes they do just the opposite. There are expectations that tend to hold us back or limit us or keep us down.

It's like something I read about flea trainers and what they have observed in the course of training fleas. Apparently, if we want to train fleas, we do it by putting them in a cardboard box with a top on it. The fleas will jump up and hit the top of the box over and over and over again. If we watch carefully, we will discover that, although the fleas continue to jump, they stop jumping high enough to hit the top. And then when the top of the box is removed, the fleas continue to jump, but they will not jump out of the box. What's the reason for this? They have conditioned themselves to jump just so high, and that's all they will do.

Expectations can be limiting and restrictive, and they can also blind us. We may be so convinced that what we expect is real, that we fail to see what actually is happening around us. Dr. Rachel Remen, in her book, *Kitchen Table Wisdom,* talks about such a scenario. She was caring for a twelve-year-old patient named Carlos, who had a dangerously low hemoglobin level. It seems that his marrow had suddenly stopped making red blood cells. The outlook was not good. In desperation, Remen tried an experimental treatment which offered a slim hope of jump-starting the marrow. It required massive doses of testosterone. The once-delightful, animated, lively twelve-year-old became sullen and short-tempered, but because his life was at stake, the treatment continued.

Remen followed his treatment closely, and monitored the results of the hemoglobin testing, which at that point in time, had a range of accuracy of 0.2. His first test was 6.0 — the same as it had been in the hospital. Then it went to 6.2, still within the error of the test method. After six weeks of the treatment, it became obvious to Dr. Remen that the medicine was not working, and it was only a matter of time before the young man would die. Week

22

after week, she looked at the current test results, and compared them to the previous week's results. She was so certain of his prognosis, that his hemoglobin had risen to 7.4 before she realized what was happening. Even then, when Remen gave the youth's mother the bad news, his mom leaned forward, touched the doctor's arm, and said, "Doctor, my boy is better, my boy is getting well!"[2] Remen had been expecting the young man to die, and that's all she saw. She had not been able to see that he was actually getting well. Like Dr. Remen, our expectations can sometimes blind us to reality.

Perhaps that's what's going on in the Bible passage we have for today. The people of the day were expecting someone — the Messiah — to come to deliver them from their suffering. It's very possible that their expectation was blinding them to the one who was right there in their midst. In fact, even John the Baptist, who had baptized Jesus, was now in prison, and seemed to be wondering if he had it all wrong. Jesus didn't seem to be fulfilling the expectations he had of what the savior was to be. Jesus didn't exactly fit the picture of what they expected in the Messiah, and he wasn't doing things the way they anticipated.

That was, in fact, true. Jesus was not acting in mighty, powerful ways. He hadn't amassed an army, nor had he broken into the political scene. Instead, he seemed to be working one by one, acting out of love, and changing lives in the process. His words and deeds cut across traditional ideas of what life, love, and faith were all about, and caused many to wonder. He just simply wasn't what people expected in terms of a savior.

This reality causes me to wonder how I would have responded had I lived during the time of Jesus. Like many of you, I often get my heart set on a certain thing, and that's what I look for, that's what I expect to find or experience. Very often, my expectations act like blinders, and I have difficulty seeing the truth that's all around me. I wonder if I could have shaken free of my expectations to see what was really happening with Jesus.

The same thing is true when it comes to this time just before Christmas. We all have expectations of what will happen this year, but I wonder if our expectations are blinding us to what's really going on? Will we see the Christ Child being born anew, or will we miss it?

I'd like to think that we could set aside all our preconceived notions about what Christmas is like, and what it's all about, and be open to see what is going on in our lives. I'd like to hope you and I could be like the little boy who was playing the role of the innkeeper in a re-enactment of the birth of Jesus. He was troubled by having to play the role, because he was the only one who had to turn Mary and Joseph away, telling them there was no room for them in the inn.

The time came for the play to be presented and it began with Joseph knocking on the door of the inn. When the young boy, turned innkeeper, opened the door, he couldn't restrain himself. He shouted at the top of his voice, "Come on in! I've been expecting you!"

May that be so for each of us this Christmas.

Closing Word

Dr. Remen talks about her home on the slopes of Mount Tamalpais in Northern California. When she moved there from Manhattan, she planted fifteen rose bushes, and expected to have a picturesque rose garden. However, after the first blooms, the roses started disappearing. Finally, she got up at dawn one morning to see what was eating the roses. She was astounded to find a magnificent 6-point stag browsing among the roses, and then choosing one of her Queen Elizabeths for breakfast! She commented: "I had thought I was planting rosebushes in order to have roses. It now seems I was actually planting rosebushes in order to have half an hour of silence with this magical animal every morning and every evening."[3]

As we look toward Christmas, I hope and pray we can expect more, much more than we ever imagined. Be ready to expect the unexpected, and go in peace. Amen.

----

1. V. S. Naipaul, *Quotable Quotes* (Pleasantville, New York: Reader's Digest, 1997), p. 67.

2. "Sleight of Hand," "I Never Promised You a Rose Garden," "Surprised by Meaning," from *Kitchen Table Wisdom* by Rachel Naomi Remen, M.D., copyright © 1996 by Rachel Naomi Remen, M.D. Used by permission of Putnam Berkley, a division of Penguin Putnam Inc.

3. *Ibid.* Used by permission.

What To Do?

Most of us have probably come to some major turning point in life when we're been trying to determine what we should do. Maybe it was trying to decide what major to declare in college, or what job to take when we finished school. Perhaps it was trying to decide whether we should move across the country to pursue our dream, or stay where we are. Many of us who have gone through seminary wrestled a lot with that decision. Was it the right thing to do? Was this what God had in mind for us?

We often struggle when it comes to our personal relationships. How do we know that this is the person with whom we should be making the commitment to spend our lives? How do we know if we should stay in the relationship, or leave it?

I know a young man, the son of some friends, who really wrestled with that decision. He had spent several years in a relationship with a woman to whom he was engaged to be married. A date was set, but the struggle went on. The young man prayed and prayed about his situation; the two young people counseled with a therapist to work through their differences. Finally, after much anxiety and heartache, the wedding was cancelled. It was so hard for them to determine what they should do, and to make the decision that was best for everyone involved.

As I was thinking about that young man, it occurred to me that what he went through was not all that different from what Joseph was experiencing in the Bible passage we have for this morning. He was confronted with a very difficult situation, and didn't know exactly what to do.

27

Just try to put yourself in his shoes. He must have felt as if he were on an emotional roller coaster! He had assumed everything was going along smoothly in his engagement to Mary, and then the bottom dropped out! At that point, he would have had to be very confused, bewildered, and torn. I'm sure there were concerns about what his family and neighbors and friends would think, and I suspect there were plenty of doubts about Mary and whether or not he could believe her. I would guess that he had his fair share of fears about what the future would hold for him, and for her.

Joseph's dilemma may not be all that different from where you and I find ourselves on occasion. Probably many of us here this morning have faced some sort of crisis in our lives, and found ourselves wondering what to do about it. What steps should we take? What is the right thing? How do we know? Looking at Joseph and seeing how he responded to his life crisis might offer us a little help in figuring it out for ourselves. Let's see what hints we can find in the story.

The first thing about Joseph is that he didn't try to be self-righteous, condemning Mary, and attempting to preserve his own reputation. Instead, he seemed to be operating out of a sense of love and compassion. Certainly he knew what the rules governing such circumstances were, and he was a guy who did the right thing. However, he was determined not to cause Mary any more disgrace. For him, relationships mattered more than rules and regulations, and he committed himself to honoring Mary to the greatest extent he could. He responded out of compassion.

Compassion is, indeed, a generous gift of love. It's easy sometimes to separate ourselves from someone we believe has done something wrong. It's easy to condemn and avoid. It's harder to put ourselves in that person's situation, and offer understanding and caring.

Compassion is the higher path. Bob Goddard once said, "Resolve to be tender with the young, compassionate with the aged, sympathetic with the striving, and tolerant with the weak and wrong. Sometime in life you will have been all of these."[1] How right he is! However, the reason for being compassionate is not so others will be compassionate toward us in return. Rather, it's the Godly thing, the loving thing to do.

We can learn from Joseph's example of compassion in all our own dealings with others. There was an article in *Parade Magazine* in the Sunday newspaper that talked about this very thing. It was about a 33-year-old all-pro linebacker for the Cleveland Browns named Chris Spielman, and how he showed compassion for his wife who was dealing with breast cancer. He was trying to make a comeback in professional football after having suffered a very serious neck injury when his wife Stephanie was diagnosed with breast cancer. Instead of making that comeback, he gave up his career in professional football to be with his wife and to care for their children. When she lost her hair from the chemotherapy treatments, Chris shaved his head. He identified with her pain and loss, and he gave a wonderful gift of love — his compassion and understanding.[2]

There's another thing Joseph did that could be helpful to us when we don't know what to do in a tough situation. He looked to God for guidance. We don't exactly read in the Bible passage that Joseph went to the synagogue to pray, nor do we read anything about his relationship with God. However, it seems obvious that he must have been a faithful man who was seeking God's guidance. If not, compassion wouldn't have been his choice. If not, he wouldn't have been receptive to hearing God's guidance through an angel in his dream. It's clear that Joseph had an ongoing relationship with God and was accepting of and responsive to the ways in which God might be speaking to him. In this case, it was in a dream.

Apparently, Joseph heeded the words he heard: "Do not be afraid to take Mary as your wife." God's direction for him was to let go of all his fears, and move forward, and that's good advice for all of us to follow.

How many times do we allow ourselves to get totally paralyzed by our fears — grounded, or ungrounded? So many of us have fears that stop us in our tracks, and we wind up doing absolutely nothing. We're stuck.

How many of us live our lives like that — paralyzed by our fears, stuck in a rut, unable to move? Fear can actually keep us from living, and it keeps us from loving. There's a book that's been out for a number of years now titled, *Love is Letting Go of Fear,* by Jampolsky. I've read it. In fact, I've even led a group that was discussing it, but I've never totally understood the significance of the title — until something happened that made it real for me.

I was out on my bike one day, and I was riding by myself. I wasn't in a terribly remote area, but there were fields that separated one house from another. As I was riding along, I saw a car pulled over to the side with the hood up. There were two guys in the car. Now my first thought was, "I should stop and see if there is anything I can do to help."

Then a small voice began to tell me, "That's foolish. What could you do? You're not a mechanic, and you don't have a phone …" As I rode on by, I realized that I was fearful; I was concerned for my safety and well-being, and didn't want to do anything stupid. However, I also realized that my fear kept me from doing what I should have done, the more loving, caring thing.

That's when I really began to understand how fear can affect us. It keeps us from being our best and most loving selves. It stunts our growth; it thwarts our love. It can cause illness. It stifles creativity. It disrupts families. We cannot allow fear to dominate our lives.

Joseph didn't do that. He heeded the word of God, and he didn't let his fears rule him. Instead, he decided what to do based on his faith in God. He married Mary, and he named the baby Jesus, as the angel had said to him. The story of Joseph is really the story of a faithful man, one who seeks and follows God's direction for his life.

That's the kind of story you and I would like to have told about our lives — a story of faithfulness. Yet that's a tough thing for many of us to attain. We want to be in control of our future, and many times, we are. However, when we run up against a brick wall, an insurmountable obstacle, a major roadblock, that's the time we come to understand that we're not in absolute control. Getting word that a son or daughter was killed in an automobile accident or hearing the dreaded word "cancer" coming from our physician can bring us to our knees.

Any life crisis can render us virtually helpless, but as Joseph knew and demonstrated, that's not the case. God is with us, no matter what. That's what faith is all about. It's putting our entire lives in God's hands, and leaning our whole weight on God. It's putting our trust in the one who will never, ever fail us.

William Arthur Ward said, "Faith is knowing there is an ocean because you have seen a brook."[3] Ralph Waldo Emerson said, "All I have seen teaches me to trust the Creator for all I have not seen."[4]

Faith is all about trust. In some ways it is like the relationship between an actor and a director. It can make or break a movie or a stage play. A professor of cinema studies was asked about the key to putting together a winning combination, and he said that it is all about trust. A director must trust that an actor has the character inside him or her, and the actor must trust a director with his or her performance. Trust — that's the key in the theater, and it's the key to faith. It just may mean taking a leap and choosing to live our lives in faith, but it really is a better way to live.

It's like one of the letters in the book, *Children's Letters To God,* that reveals a childlike trust. It's from a little girl named Nora, and it goes like this: "Dear God, I don't ever feel alone since I found out about you."[5] That's what faith is. Joseph had it, and so can we.

Closing Word

A while back, I spent the weekend in New York with my husband who was working there for a few days. During the time that I was there, there was a problem in Times Square. The CondeNast building was under construction, and a crane working on the building had a problem of some sort that caused the scaffolding to collapse. The whole area was cordoned off to traffic and the public while the crews tried to put up a huge net around the building to secure it and to catch any falling debris.

That's what it means to have trust in God. Faith in God is like having a huge net that catches us when we fall, and holds us up when we can't stand on our own. As you leave here this morning, trust in God, and go in peace. Amen.

---

1. Bob Goddard, *Quotable Quotes* (Pleasantville, New York: 1997), p. 77.

2. "A Tale Of Two Comebacks," by Dick Schaap, which appeared in the September 12, 1999 issue of *Parade*. Used with permission from Parade, copyright © 1999.

3. William Arthur Ward, *Quotable Quotes* (Pleasantville, New York: Reader's Digest, 1997), p. 153.

4. Ralph Waldo Emerson, *Quotable Quotes* (Pleasantville, New York: Reader's Digest, 1997), p. 153.

5. Stuart Hample & Eric Marshall, *Children's Letters To God* (New York: Workman Publishing, 1991).

Good News!

A young girl was driving around the city with her family, looking at the various displays of Christmas lights. They passed a church that had a beautifully lit nativity scene, so they parked the car and got out to look at it more closely. They all "oo-ed" and "ah-ed," and the little girl's grandmother said, "Isn't it beautiful?" "Yes, Grandma, it's really nice," the little girl said. "But isn't baby Jesus ever going to grow up? He's the same size he was last year!"[1]

Do you ever have that feeling when it comes to Christmas? Kind of "been there, done that"? It's the same thing, the same way, year after year. It's the same old story, often told in the same way, and nothing seems to change. There doesn't seem to be anything new or different, or any growth or change that has come since the last time we heard it.

To be honest, Christmas is a tough one, and designing a Christmas Eve service often seems to be difficult. It's hard because we have memories of what has been; we have our ideas of what we want it to be and what we think it should be. Probably a lot of us have traditions around Christmas and Christmas Eve that we value and want to preserve.

Sometimes, it's the same old story, and the same familiar songs, and they seem to be empty. For whatever reason, Christmas doesn't ring true; it doesn't seem real. It doesn't connect with us in a way that makes any difference. In truth, it can feel quite meaningless.

I'd be willing to bet we're all here because we want to believe that the event we remember and celebrate tonight is important. We want to believe it matters. We need it to make a difference in our lives, and not just be something from 2,000 years ago. We want it to be very real for you and for me, right here, right now.

There are really a number of ways we can view Christmas, but for Christians around the world, it is seen as "the birth of God on earth." That's what we proclaim happened at Christmas. This is the anniversary of the appearance of the God of the universe in the form of a helpless baby, and it is, indeed, a really important day, and worthy of reverence and celebration.

Stop to think about it. That's a remarkable thing! I've always referred to Christmas as God's ultimate public relations campaign, because I understand Christmas as God's attempt to get through to us. God has always been a God of relationship, a God who wants us to draw close, to love and be loved.

However, the history of humanity is that we never quite get it. As human beings, we keep messing things up. The birth of Jesus, God in human form, was God's way of breaking through to us, God's way of getting our attention by communicating a love that supersedes anything we ever imagined possible. Only God could have envisioned this way of attracting us — not coming as a powerful military ruler, or a mighty king, in the conventional sense. God didn't choose to come to us in a way that overwhelmed us, or overpowered us, or caused us to respond out of fear.

Instead, God came in total innocence and helplessness, as a newborn infant. Think about our response to a new baby. I can't see one without feeling awestruck. Have you ever looked at those tiny fingernails? Have you ever touched that baby-soft skin? Have you ever looked at those wisps of hair, or the almost-invisible eyelashes of a newborn baby? It certainly seems miraculous to me!

Have you ever noticed how most people respond to a baby? Even the most hardened curmudgeon has a tough time not smiling at a baby. It's hard not to go over to a baby and begin making all kinds of "goo-goo" noises and sounds. A baby draws us in, and that's precisely why God came in human form on this earth — to draw us closer.

In some ways, I see Christmas and God like a story another pastor told. He was at a dinner party during the Christmas season. The house was beautifully decorated, and there was an electric

34

train set up around the base of the Christmas tree. One of the children was running the train too fast, and it derailed. She was bent over trying to put it back on the track, when the host noticed what she was doing and went over to help. He said to her, "You can't do that from above; you have to get down beside it." Then he lay down on the floor beside the train where he could see to place it back on its track.[2]

Maybe that's what God did at Christmas. Perhaps the Christmas story is God's attempt to lie down beside us, to see and experience life as we see it, to draw close to us in a way we can understand. It's God's continuing to reach out to us, again, and again, and again.

That's the really good news of Christmas. Yes, we are celebrating a wondrous event that we believe really did happen thousands of years ago, but that's not all. We are also celebrating that Christmas can happen again, right here, right now, in our hearts and in our homes. God can be born again this night.

This story isn't just a one-time thing. It's God's promise always to be there, to be with us, within us, among us, right now, tonight. It isn't just something that happened once a lot of years ago. It's something that can happen right now. God's love can happen to us on this night in December or some balmy night in mid-July. It can be real for us at any moment in life. Christmas is just the reminder of that.

It's like something that Bert Holloway of Cambridge, England, understands. Every year for 43 years, at one minute after midnight on Christmas Eve, Bert has handed his wife Ethel a love letter. The gift is a tradition they started when they were first married, and every year he reaffirms his love for her in letters she keeps and treasures.[3]

I think that's what Christmas is meant to be for us — God's yearly love letter, God's reminder and reaffirmation of unconditional, undying love. Tonight we have the opportunity to open that letter again, and we can treasure all that it holds in our hearts.

Christmas is God coming to us in the form of Jesus, and offering us more than we ever believed possible. Jesus brings us all the hope and possibility we see in a newborn babe. Jesus shows us the incredible love God has for each of us, and affirms that light can break through even the darkest night to brighten our world.

Maybe the truth of Christmas will really break through to each of us this year, as it did in a story I received on e-mail about some children in a Russian orphanage. Two Americans were in Russia by invitation from the Department of Education, and they were there to teach morals and ethics in prisons and businesses, in the fire and police departments, and in a large orphanage.

During the holiday season of 1994, the two visitors told the children in the orphanage the traditional story of Christmas. The children heard all about how Mary and Joseph went to Bethlehem, and finding no room in the inn, spent the night in a stable. They heard how Jesus was born there and placed in a manger.

The children were enthralled with the story, and after it was told, they were given a small piece of cardboard to make a manger, and some scraps of paper to make straw for the manger. The Americans also had some pieces of material for the children to use as the blanket, and some felt material to be fashioned into the baby Jesus.

The adults walked among the children as they were making their own version of the nativity scene, just to see if they needed any help. Everything was going well, until they got to the table where a little six-year-old named Misha was sitting. As the teacher looked into his manger, she was surprised to see two babies in the manger, instead of just one.

Very quickly, the translator was summoned, and the child was asked why there were two babies in the manger. With his arms crossed in front of him, little Misha began to retell the story he had heard for the first time just moments before. He had all the happenings accurately, until he got to the part where Mary put the baby Jesus in the manger.

It was then that he began to ad-lib, making up his own ending to the story. His version went like this: "When Maria laid the baby in the manger, Jesus looked at me and asked me if I had a place to stay. I told him I have no mamma and I have no papa, so I don't have any place to stay. Then Jesus told me I could stay with him. But I told him I couldn't, because I didn't have a gift to give him like everybody else did. But I wanted to stay with Jesus so much, so I thought about what I had that maybe I could use for a gift. I thought maybe if I kept him warm, that would be a good gift. So I asked Jesus, 'If I keep you warm, will that be a good enough gift?' and Jesus said that would be the best gift anybody ever gave him. So I got into the manger, and then Jesus looked at me and he told me I could stay with him — for always."[4]

That's what happens at Christmas. Jesus, God in the flesh, is born among us, and is with us always. That's what we remember and celebrate tonight as we light our candles and carry the light of the love of Jesus out into the world. God can be born again, this very moment, and God's love can break through once again to change you, to change me, to change the world.

Closing Word

As you leave here tonight, carry the light of the love of God in Christ Jesus into the world. Have a Merry Christmas, and go in peace. Amen.

---

1. "Christmas," *Dynamic Illustrations,* Nov/Dec 94.

2. "Christmas," *Dynamic Illustrations,* Nov/Dec 92.

3. Bert Holloway, "Advent," *Dynamic Illustrations,* Nov/Dec 96.

4. e-mail, "Taking The Christmas Story To Heart," received Dec 98.

The Power Of A Dream

Do you dream? Do you remember your dreams? I remember a number of years ago when I was leading a women's study group, and someone wanted to read and study about dreams. I wasn't too eager to pursue the idea, because I wasn't convinced that a study of dreams had much merit. Nonetheless, the group persisted, and we chose a book about dreams whose title I've long since forgotten. We set about reading and discussing it, and I began to become a bit more open to the possibility that dreams can be a way for God to get through to us, and they can literally change and redirect our lives.

If we study the Bible closely, we can clearly see that dreams have great significance, and can be ways for God to speak. That's certainly a very valid way to understand and interpret what we find in the Bible passage that we have for today. There are three different times in the story of Joseph and Mary and the baby and their flight to Egypt that we are told that Joseph heard from God via a dream. First, he had a dream that an angel came to him, and told him to go to Egypt to escape the wrath of Herod. Later on, an angel came to him in a dream, telling him to go back to Israel, and a third time he received direction in a dream to settle in the area of Galilee. And each time, we either read or see evidence of the fact that Joseph obeyed the instruction he had received in the dream. Clearly, he believed that dreams were a way for God to speak to him, to reveal a purpose for his life and to give him a sense of direction. Throughout the ages, that has been an accepted understanding of dreams and their significance.

Does it still work today? Does God, in fact, "speak" to us through dreams? While I'm certainly not an expert on the matter, I would have to say, "Yes, God can and does use dreams to communicate with us." The real issue has to do with discerning what dreams are of God, and what dreams are merely provoked by the things we've just experienced in our lives, or some sense of wishful thinking. I believe that all of our dreams have the potential to reveal our deepest longings and passions, and to reveal God's will for our lives.

Fortunately, there are many others who have spoken about the power of a dream — whether that be an actual dream while we're sleeping, or some God-inspired revelation or desire. For example, Walt Kallestad, pastor of Community Church of Joy in Glendale, Arizona, has written a book titled, *Wake Up Your Dreams*. In it, he says things like: "One 'small' dream set in motion is powerful enough to unleash the potential in other dreamers and, dream by dream, to reshape the world."[1] He also writes, "Dreams can help us see the invisible, believe the incredible, and achieve the impossible."[2]

Dreams are important, because they are guideposts to a future that is, as yet, unseen. Dreams are important because they are life-giving, and because they can be revelations from God. They can point us toward what God is calling us to be or to do. They can fill us with energy and hope. When we have dreams, we have life.

A dream gives us a reason for being, a sense of purpose and meaning for our lives. Dreams can give us a picture of the future, and they can inspire. They lead us to reach higher, and be more than we thought we could be. They lead us to new, unheard-of horizons. They give us energy and hope that a new future, a preferred future, in fact, come into being.

You're probably thinking that I've totally lost it with all this dream stuff! As I stated earlier, I used to be a real skeptic about all this. I firmly asserted that I never dreamed, and, even if I did, I certainly could never remember my dreams. Even if I remembered, they could be completely justified by something I'd read or recently experienced. However, I've had three different experiences that have changed all that. Two of them occurred after the deaths of my parents, and I'll share them another time. But the one I want to tell you about this morning is one that has direct bearing on the ministry in which I'm spending my life — THE GARDEN.

It happened in November of 1994. For months prior to this time, I had been wrestling with where God wanted me to be in ministry. I was considering the possibility of leaving pastoral ministry, and pursuing some other venture. I had been in conversation with the placement personnel of our denomination about moving to another church, and another appointment, but it just didn't work out. Nothing seemed to be right.

This may come as a surprise to some of you, but the church has a very political nature, and advancement often comes with moves, and many pastors get caught up in "moving up" in the system, and making it into one of the top churches. I'm not very proud to say that I was getting myself caught in that, and I was in constant turmoil wondering what I'd be offered. Would it be all right? Would it offer sufficient advancement opportunities?

I had just left some of that behind in Indianapolis, and was on a flight winging my way west to conduct some interviews as part of my doctoral studies. A colleague was flying there with me, but he had gone to sleep. I had been reading, and decided that I, too, would stretch out and take a little nap.

I can't tell you exactly what happened, but I dreamed about the story I had just been reading in a book by Tom Peters about the invention of Nintendo. I don't think I slept very long, but when I woke up, I knew exactly what I was supposed to be doing in my ministry. I felt an amazing sense of calm, and all the turmoil I had experienced over the last few months had virtually evaporated.

I leaned over to my fellow traveler, and said, "Steve, I've had a revelation from God. I know what I'm supposed to do in ministry." He thought I was sick or something, since this didn't sound like the Linda McCoy he knew, but I knew it was for real. That sense of calm has never left me, and the vision was clear. That dream was God's planting the beginning vision for what we now call THE GARDEN.

As a result of that dream, many of us have experienced a whole new insurgence of the love of God. Empowered with the incredible energy of God, many of us have reached beyond our wildest dreams.

I don't think I'm the only one in this room this morning who is firmly convinced that dreams are God-given. We know they are powerful, and they can come true.

Closing Word

Probably the most well known address about having a dream is the speech by Dr. Martin Luther King, Jr., during a civil rights march on Washington on August 28, 1963. Listen to what he said:

> *I say to you today, my friends, that in spite of the difficulties and frustrations of the moment, I still have a dream ... I have a dream that one day this nation will rise up and live out the true meaning of its creed ... I have a dream that my four little children will one day live in a nation where they will not be judged by the color of their skin but by the content of their character. I have a dream that one day every valley shall be exalted, every hill and mountain shall be made low, the rough places will be made plain, and the crooked places will be made straight, and the glory of the Lord shall be revealed, and all flesh shall see it together....*[3]

Do you have a dream? Do you have a dream that one day, you'll be living as you're called to live? Do you have a dream that God is trying to communicate to you?

As we leave here this morning, may God speak to each of us. Let us open our hearts to our deepest dreams. Hold onto them; reach higher; know they can come true; and go in peace. Amen.

---

1. Walt Kallestad, *Wake Up Your Dreams* (Grand Rapids, Michigan: Zondervan Publishing House, 1996), p. 17.

2. *Ibid.*, p. 23

3. Dr. Martin Luther King, Jr., "I Have a Dream," delivered on the steps of the Lincoln Memorial in Washington, D.C., on August 28, 1963.

Christmas 2
John 1:(1-9) 10-18

Show And Tell

An article in *U. S. News and World Report* stated that 93 percent of Americans believe in God or in some sort of universal spirit that can be put in the same category as God. Those statistics appear from time to time in a Gallup Poll or some other poll. Although they vary a bit, they all point to the fact that Americans believe in God.

The problem is that we humans are really almost incapable of grasping the magnitude, the depth, the breadth, the limitlessness of God. It's impossible to capture the essence of God in any image or metaphor. In some ways, it's like getting some ocean water in a jar and proclaiming that it represents the fullness of the ocean itself. We know that the little jar of water is merely a hint of the nature of the ocean, but there is much that is lost in the jar — the waves, the tide, the roar, the soothing ebb and flow, the glint of sun on the waters, the white foam as the waves break, the creatures living beneath the sea.

I fear the same thing may happen when we try to put words to trying to describe who God is and what God is like. Nonetheless, there is a lot of curiosity about God. You've probably heard about the family that arrived home from the hospital with their new little baby. They were putting him to bed, and his older brother was insistent that he needed to spend some time with the baby — all by himself. The parents were a bit apprehensive about what the older brother might do, so they stood at the door and watched and listened as the little boy went into the room. He tiptoed up to the crib, leaned as close as he could to the baby, and whispered, "Quick, little brother, before you forget, tell me what God's like."

I guess it's just a part of human nature that we have our questions about God, wondering who God is, and what God is like. You may know the name of Robert Coles, a well-known author and child psychiatrist, who wrote *The Spiritual Life of Children* a few years ago. In it, he shares some of their insights about God, religion, and the ultimate meaning of life. When asked what God looks like, one child named Barry Wormser drew a picture of God and said God is "half boy, half girl, sometimes happy, sometimes sad." Twelve-year-old J. R. Cohee said, "I've always thought he's made up of clouds ,.." Ten-year-old Jennifer Anderson said, "I don't imagine God as a person. I imagine him as air."[1]

If we look at our Bible passage for today, we may discover that some of the writers from the past may be closer to the truth than we normally think. This passage is affirming the reality that Jesus is God in human form. Jesus lived as we do, experienced what we experience, shared the same joys and sorrows that we share. Jesus was God in the flesh, right here among us. By being God in the flesh, Jesus was the ultimate revelation of what God is really like. That means that we can look at the life of Jesus and come to some understanding of the nature of God, and that's what I'd like to spend some time thinking about with you this morning.

First, I believe Jesus points toward a God who is personal and intimate, and who cares for you and me in a very deep way. At one point, Jesus prays to God, and addresses God as "Papa, Father." In Aramaic, which is the language Jesus spoke, the word he used was "Abba." By using this word, Jesus was not inferring that God was male, but rather he used "Abba" to indicate the nature of the relationship with God. "Abba" is really closer in meaning to "Daddy" than anything else, and was meant to show that relationship with God is something that is close and intimate. That says that God is right here with us, and is active in our lives and in our world.

There's a balancing factor to that understanding of God with us and among us. Our Bible passage this morning also affirms that God is creator, the one who started everything. It hearkens back to the creation story in Genesis, and forms one of my very basic understandings of the nature of God. God is the source of all of life, the beginning, the first, the one who existed before anything or anyone else. I don't read the creation story as an accurate account of exactly how creation occurred, and so, in that regard, I have problems understanding those who somehow think there's a conflict between the creation story and the scientist's evolution or big bang theories of creation. As I understand it, the creation story doesn't tell us how, but who. It tells us the source, the one behind all of creation.

God as Creator has an impact on our lives. It means that every time we get a new idea, or have an insight into a plaguing problem, every time something new or fresh comes into being, that's the creative activity of God at work. God as creator, God as the source, the beginning, can be an awe-inspiring concept.

There's more that Jesus and this Bible passage tell us about the nature of God. Jesus demonstrates God's lovingkindness (grace) toward us and acceptance and love of us. I really like the images theologian Sallie McFague uses in one of her books to describe God. She calls God "Mother-Father God," and she refers to God as Lover, and as Friend.[2]

Mother-Father God gives us the same sense of God as "Abba" did for Jesus. But for me, God as Lover is the most radical, powerful image! Can't you just imagine what it feels like to be loved by the Ultimate Lover? It means being affirmed, accepted, loved just as we are! I don't know about you, but this is the image of God I most want to embrace — God as Lover, or what a child once described as "the huggy God."

Another part of the nature of God which is clear to me in this passage and through Jesus is that God is a seeking God — always seeking us out, trying to connect with us. That is why God chose to come to us in the flesh, to get through to us, to connect with us in a way that wasn't possible if we only regarded God as remote and impersonal.

In fact, I wonder if God isn't a little like a Welshman I read about who for forty years went to his neighbor's door each week and slipped a love letter underneath it. The two had had an argument years before, and she refused to speak to him. Finally, after writing 2,184 love letters with no response of any kind, the 74-year-old man went to the door, knocked on it, and asked the 74-year-old woman to marry him. She said, "Yes." I think God is a lot like that, slipping us love notes, and knocking on our door, waiting for us to open it, and say, "Yes."

It is difficult to try to define the nature of God. For me, God is not some distant, remote deity, but is rather very much a part of who we are and how we live. The spirit of God is as close to us as the air we breathe; God is all around us and in us. I believe that God is not so much apart from us as a part of us. Within each of us is some spark of the divine, the holy. It's like something theologian Paul Tillich suggested. He thought that we must abandon the idea of an external God far removed from us, and replace that image with one of God as the inner sense of being centered and grounded.

In reality, none of this theological jargon really matters. What really counts is the experience you and I have of the holy in our own lives. Let me share one of the most powerful experiences I've ever been through. It happened at a world gathering of clergywomen a number of years ago. We were experiencing a Native American worship service, and in the course of that service, two women walked around the room, one of them carrying a bowl that had something burning in it. The other carried a feather, which she was waving, sending the smoke wafting into the air, around and over us.

As that was happening, someone began singing a song that begins, "Spirit of the living God, fall afresh on me ... spirit of the living God, fall afresh on me." My experience of God took on a whole new dimension in that moment! God was no longer some external power or force, but was in me and around me. I don't think I'd ever been so connected with God, before or since.

Experiencing God may be a little like listening to our favorite music played through a magnificent sound system. We can't touch or see it, and it can't be confined to one place. It permeates everything. It's very real, and touches us at the depth of our being. I wonder if that isn't more what God is like.

46

Closing Word

Someone named Carlo Carretto shared his understanding of the nature of God when he said, "Human experience is already experience of God. Our journey on earth is already a journey to heaven. Seeing a sunrise or a flower is already seeing God."[3]

As you leave here this morning, know that God goes before us, behind us, above us, below us. Know that God is within us. We are a part of God, and God is a part of us. So go in peace. Amen.

---

1. Robert Coles, *Spiritual Life of Children* (Boston: Houghton Mifflin Company, 1990).

2. Sallie McFague, *Models of God: Theology for an Ecological, Nuclear Age* (Philadelphia: Fortress Press, 1989), pp. 84-85.

3. Rosalie Maggio, editor, *Quotations For The Soul* (Paramus, New Jersey: Prentice Hall, 1997), p. 77.

A God Thing

Bil Keane, the creator of the *Family Circus* cartoon, said he was drawing a cartoon one day when his little boy came in and asked, "Daddy, how do you know what to draw?" Keane replied, "God tells me." Then the boy asked, "Then why do you keep erasing parts of it?"[1]

The child brings up an interesting point. Does God tell Bil Keane what to draw? Conversations like that one evoke all kinds of questions in us. It's like a discussion our worship team got into one night about whether or not God "talks" to us, or if it's just us talking to ourselves, or some coincidence, or nothing at all. If we're trying to make a decision, and we ask God for guidance, how do we know if the choice we make is God's direction for us or not? How clear cut is it?

I've often said I wish there were a bell that rang, and an announcement that said, "God now speaking. Pay attention." Or someone going, "Yoo-hoo, yoo-hoo, God here ..." I guess what most of us would really like is Caller ID, some clear, obvious sign that the direction we're going, or the path we're taking is the way that's right for us. How do we in fact know that it's a "God thing"?

Jesus certainly seemed to know in our Bible passage for today. There are many approaches we could take to this particular passage, but the thought that occurred to me repeatedly as I read and studied it was, "How did he know it was God's voice?" I realize that Jesus was a lot more closely attuned to God than you and I are, but I still wonder if God speaks to us, too. If so, how do we know? How do we know that what we're doing is the right thing, the God thing? Do we hear voices, or like Moses, have burning bush encounters in this day and age? If we were to tell someone God spoke to us in the middle of our busy day by setting the papers on our desk on fire, and not turning them to ashes, would anybody believe us, or would we be committed somewhere?

When I was preparing for ministry, one of the exams we had to take was the Minnesota Multiphasic Personality Inventory, or the MMPI. There are 600-some questions on that testing tool, and they keep repeating themselves. One of the repeaters has to do with hearing the voice of God, and that's one of the things that's used to weed out the questionable, unhealthy candidates for the ministry. Strange as it may seem, it's considered psychologically unhealthy to say you've heard the voice of God.

So then, does God speak to us? Today? Here? If so, how does that happen? Is it real, or are we crazy to think so? That's the question author Dan Wakefield asks in his book, *How Do We Know When It's God?* He recounts a long spiritual journey, and tells of the many times he was caught in a dilemma, and sought God's guidance. Should he go to California to write a movie script, or should he stay on the East Coast? Should he attend this seminar, or that one? Should he commit to this relationship, or wait? He talks about desperately seeking a sign of some sort that would let him know for sure that God is there, directing and guiding him, casting light in his darkness, showing him the way. "How do we know when it's God?"[2]

I'm convinced that God does indeed speak to us and interact with us, but I think I need to back up a little and tell you some of the basic beliefs I hold about God that support my conviction.

First, I believe God is in everything and is everywhere. As a friend put it, "There's not a spot where God is not." Other writers have expressed the same thought. Harriet Martineau said, "There's nothing which is not full of God."[3] Baruch Spinoza said, "Whatever is, is in God."[4] And Meister Eckhart said, "Apprehend God in all things, for God is in all things."[5]

Do you see what it means for God to be everywhere and in everything? It means that God really does speak to us, but the voice can come in a myriad of forms. Maybe it's that gut feeling that leads us one direction instead of another. Perhaps we are hearing the voice of God when we start asking questions that we've never asked before. Maybe it's when an idea comes to us that we've never considered before, or maybe it's a random thought that just keeps nagging us. Maybe it occurs through hearing a piece of music, or in our imaginations, or through our dreams. Maybe it's God's voice that says to us through a friend, "Have you ever thought about...?" — words that plant a notion in our minds that we never thought about before.

I've also come to realize that there really are no coincidences in life. The people who are in our lives right now are people who are part of our spiritual journey. What are we learning from them? How are they God in our lives? When things seem to come together serendipitously, I've begun to pay more attention. If someone comes to me, for instance, and talks about something that I've just read about, or about something someone else has just mentioned, I try to listen. I believe that's the voice of God trying to get through to us. I believe God is everywhere, and is in everything.

There's a second thing about God that's very much connected with the first. Not only is God everywhere, but God is active everywhere. I do not believe God is some distant idea or concept, or some remote being. Instead, God is a very real, a very present, a very active force in our world and in our lives, if we allow that to be the case. God is always active bringing a new thing.

Allow me to clarify something here. When I say God is active, I do not mean that God is orchestrating everything that happens, or causing everything that occurs in our lives. I don't believe God puts us in certain circumstances or hardships, or causes us to be in this place and not that place. God doesn't cause or send illness or disaster, and I don't believe that God's activity in those kinds of situations means there will be the sudden suspension of a tornado or a miraculous healing.

Rather, I think God is active in and works through every experience and every person we encounter in life to bring out the good in even the worst of situations. God knows our disappointments, and failures, our heartaches, and our fears, and I firmly believe

God can be at work in the midst of the bad times, bringing possibility and hope out of them. I'm convinced the reassuring voice of God is calling to us, through the hug of a friend, or a word of encouragement, or a much-needed phone call. God is active and present in our lives.

That brings us to the third thing I believe about God, and that is, without any doubt, God is good. Period. End of conversation. That for me is the litmus test for whether or not the nudges we feel, the ideas we get, the experiences that come our way are of God or not. The ultimate test is asking the question: "Are these ideas positive and good? Are they life-giving?" Obviously, the idea to rob a bank is not of God because it does not meet the test of being a good, positive, life-giving option for a direction to choose. The way we can tell if it's a God thing or not is whether or not it is good.

There are probably some of you here this morning thinking, "I've never had anything like the Jesus thing happen to me. Not one of those super-duper, extraordinary, supernatural things has ever occurred in my life! God's certainly never spoken to me."

I'm not trying to say that type of experience of God is something we must all go through. I know those kinds of peak experiences, those ah-ha moments happen, but not every time, and not to everyone. Sometimes that isn't the best way for God to get through to us, and sometimes we just aren't open or ready for these kinds of experiences.

I also know there are times that, no matter how much we want it or think we're searching for connection with God, it doesn't happen. I believe God is always present, always with us, but I think there are times when, for whatever reason, we just can't connect. We can't see or hear God in our lives or anywhere else.

I have a friend who feels that God is absent from his life right now. He's always experienced God's presence and direction for his life through nature, but that's not doing it for him. The ocean where he's heard the voice of God is silent. The birds aren't singing anymore for him.

That probably happens to all of us at one time or another. We all go through stages and phases and changes and transitions in our lives, and the ways that once connected us to God may not work for us now. Maybe we've even been so beaten down or so roughed up by life, that we're callused and hardened, and we can't see God's presence or hear God's voice in our lives.

Nonetheless, I'm convinced God is there, and keeps trying to connect with us in ways we can understand. For my friend, I wonder if it's by way of the new connections he's made with a couple of folks on the Internet. Maybe not, but if they meet the test of being good, positive, and life-giving, they just might be God in his life right now.

How do we know it's a God thing? How do we know it's God who is speaking to us and leading us? Sometimes it may come in the way it did for Jesus — through a powerful, life-changing, clear-cut experience. For some of us, it may occur in the ordinary, everyday routines when we sense God's presence in one clear, shining moment.

I was thinking back to how I wound up in ministry. It wasn't a big, cataclysmic kind of thing, but I believe it was very much a God thing. For me, it was a slowly unfolding process that all began with the sense of a pull, a nudge, a thought that seemed to be drawing me in a certain direction. It culminated in my asking a rather innocent question of a good friend who happened to be a pastor. It was a question along the lines of "What would it be like to go to seminary?" You can figure out the rest of the story.

So, is God speaking to you in your life? Have you heard God's voice? Let me tell you, God is everywhere and in everything, and God is active doing a new thing. And if it's a good thing, you can trust that it's a God thing.

Closing Word

I've come to believe that the key question isn't really whether or not God speaks to us, because I'm convinced God is constantly trying to connect with us. Maybe the key question is "Are we listening? Are we looking for God in our world? Are we expecting God to be active in our lives?"

As you leave here this morning, try to tune in to what God just might be saying to you. And go in peace. Amen.

1. Cal and Rose Samra, *Holy Humor* (Portage, Michigan: Fellowship of Merry Christians, Inc., 1996), pp. 22-23.

2. Dan Wakefield, *How Do We Know When It's God?* (Boston/London/New York: Little, Brown and Company, 1999), p. 68-69.

3. Rosalie Maggio, editor, *Quotations For The Soul* (Paramus, New Jersey: Prentice Hall, 1997), p. 20.

4. *Ibid.*, p. 18.

5. *Ibid.*, p. 19.

Positive Identification

A while ago, I received an invitation to my high school reunion. Now I'm not going to tell you which one, but I've been out of high school for a while. At any rate, getting that invitation took me back to those days in Madison, Indiana, and caused me to think about some of the people who were in my class. I began wondering where they are, and what they're doing. I know about three of them: one is mayor of Madison, and another is the editor and owner of the newspaper, and one teaches classes to those who want to become nurses.

I guess that all doesn't really matter, but because of that reunion announcement, I caught myself remembering certain moments or events that happened during high school and thinking back to what we were like then — the people we were, or at least who we thought we were. What I realized is just how much our past shapes us and helps determine who we are today. I like to think I'm quite different from the person I was back then, and I know I am in a lot of ways. However, I'm also aware that much of who I am at the core of my being is very much linked to those growing up days in Madison.

Trying to figure out who we are is a struggle for many of us. We keep searching, trying to get some sense of our identity. Did you know that there's a course at Stanford University's Graduate School of Business that's entitled, "Who am I?" That's how important, basic, and elusive, the answer to that question seems to be.

We've probably all read about or heard about those quests to determine a positive identification. Not long ago, we read about the DNA testing on the remains in the tomb of the Unknown Soldier to determine who it was. The tests did confirm an identity, and the young man who had died in Vietnam was given the burial his family so wanted him to have.

It may be like a story I read about a family who had gone to the movies, and on the way in the young man of the group stopped by the refreshment stand to pick up some popcorn. By the time he got into the theater, the lights were already dim, and the theater was darkened. He looked over everyone in the place, but simply couldn't find his family. Finally, after wandering up and down the aisles several times searching the crowd in the darkness, he stopped and asked out loud, "Does anyone recognize me?"

In some ways, we're all asking the same kind of question. "Does anyone recognize me? Does anyone know who I am?" We want to know who we are. It's as though we have to know who we are before we can know anything else. Understanding who we are seems to be the basic underlying question from which everything else flows, and it's something for which we keep searching.

Trying to establish identities and figure out who people are is precisely what's going on in the Bible passage we have for today. Throughout the entire passage, one person or another is attempting to put a label or a title on Jesus to determine exactly who he is. We find things like "God's Passover Lamb," "God-Revealer," "Son of God," "Rabbi," and "Messiah" as terms that are assigned to him.

Often we do the same thing when we meet new people. There's always the desire to know who that person is, and we often believe that a title or a name will tell us that. I've had a few interesting things happen when I've been asked the question, "What do you do?" Often my response brings a "Really? That's nice."

However, that's not always the response I get. One time a few years ago, I had been asked to give the opening prayer at the Economic Club luncheon downtown. Prior to the start of the meeting, I was milling around in the hall outside the banquet room, and ran into some people I knew. They introduced me to another person who was with them by saying, "Linda is one of the pastors at our church." This other person looked me in the eye, and said, "I don't approve of women ministers." Needless to say, that ended that conversation.

Sometimes, I'd really like to do what Robert Fulghum does when someone asks him the question, "What do you do for a living?" He makes something up. Now usually, if you stretch it a bit, his answer is based on some thread of truth, but it isn't actually what he does to earn money. For example, he had to fill out a form at the bank one day, and there was a blank for his occupation. So he wrote down "prince." He said that just that morning his wife had said to him, "Fulghum, sometimes you are a real prince." And he was feeling rather princely that day, so he responded that he was a prince. The bank teller couldn't handle it, and they had a little debate on the matter of identity, and whether our identity has to do with our occupation — what we get paid for, or whether it's something greater than that.[1]

Trying to establish positive identification is what the Bible passage for this morning is all about. We've seen the attempts to determine who Jesus actually was by putting titles and names on him. The most interesting part of this passage to me, however, is at the very end when Simon comes to Jesus. The first thing Jesus says to him is, "You're John's son, Simon?" He's trying to get clear on who he is by knowing whose son he is, but Jesus doesn't stop there. He gives Simon a new name, or a nickname, saying he'll be called "Cephas," Peter, from now on. Cephas means "Rock."

In looking back at scripture, we discover that being given a new name or undergoing a name change could be highly significant. It often signifies a radical change in the person, and in who that person is, that comes as a result of an encounter with the Holy. That was the case with Abram and Sarai becoming Abraham and Sarah. That was true with Saul when he became Paul. Their new names reflected that they had become new beings because they had an encounter with the Divine. I think a similar thing is happening here.

In some very real ways, renaming Simon as Peter, the Rock, tells us who he is. "Rock" represents something that is solid, durable, strong. It can be the foundation upon which something else

57

is built. It seems that using the name "Rock" for Simon Peter really tells us a lot about who he is, his character, and the person he is becoming because he has had a real encounter with Jesus.

In the same way, I really believe that none of us knows who we really are unless and until we open ourselves to the light of God, who reveals to us our true identity. I'm convinced that at the heart of it all, we will discover that each one of us is a child of God, loved by God, created by God.

That's at the core of my faith. A lot of my faith journey is connected to an understanding of who I am. In my "other" life, I was a junior high school French teacher, Madame McCoy to my students. I really felt as though I knew who I was when I was teaching. Our daughter is adopted, and she came to us literally overnight, in 24 hours and 30 minutes time. One day I was teaching, and the next, I was a mother.

You need to understand that we wanted to have a child very badly, and we loved and love her dearly. But I went through some real struggles, an identity crisis really, during those first few months as I tried to figure out who I was *now*. There was no paycheck, no Madame McCoy, seemingly no identity.

About that same time I got involved in a Bible study group, and I began to wrestle with what was going on in me. Slowly, but surely, it began to dawn on me that my identity didn't have anything to do with my role or job or title. It didn't have anything to do with what I looked like, or what anyone else thought of me. If all that were stripped away, and it could be, it finally sank in that I am Linda McCoy, child of God, loved by God. That's who I am, and that's all I need to know.

The same is true for each one of us. Each of us is a child of God, and God loves each one of us more than we can ever imagine. Each one of us can know who we are. We can say with assurance, "God, I am your child." That's who we are.

Closing Word

I had some new cards printed the other day. Guess what they say? "Linda McCoy, Child of God." Here ... want one?

On the tables are some cards for you to fill out and carry with you. There's a blank where you can put your name, and underneath the blank is the title that fits us all — "Child of God." That's our positive ID.

As you leave here this morning, know who you are — a child of God — and go in peace. Amen.

---

1. *It Was On Fire When I Lay Down On It*, by Robert L. Fulghum, copyright 1988, 1989. Used by permission of Villard Books, a Division of Random House Inc.

Answering The Call

A few years ago, I was on a retreat in northern Michigan, and I knew that some of our friends from home were sailing in the vicinity. One evening I went to the local boat dock, and walked through the lines of boats calling out the names of our friends, hopeful that they might be there. I remember the joy I felt when I yelled their names, and they answered! They were actually there, and they responded to my call!

However, there are times when we get a call that we don't hear, or don't want to hear. It might be a matter of thinking, "My plate is already full. Call back tomorrow." There are times that we don't even answer the call, especially if we don't know who's calling. That's true these days with "Caller ID" that can be put on our phones, identifying the person who's placing the call to us. Sometimes we don't answer the call because we're not home, or because we don't hear the call come in. There are a variety of reasons that many of us don't answer a call when it comes to us.

I think that's part of what makes the Bible passage for today so remarkable. Now, granted, we're not talking about a phone call from an unknown source; we're talking about a face-to-face encounter. Nonetheless, I've always found the story of Jesus calling his first group of followers to be something worthy of our attention.

Think about that part of the Bible passage with me. Here we have four guys; two sets of brothers, doing what they normally did — fishing in the Sea of Galilee. Now, who knows? Maybe they didn't really enjoy what they were doing. Perhaps they were fishing because that's just what you did for a living when you lived in that region. Maybe they did it because that's what their family determined was in their future. Or maybe they did it because they genuinely enjoyed the outdoors and the challenge of bringing in a load of fish each day.

We don't know for sure why they were doing what they were doing, nor do we know how they felt about it. We only know that they were doing their normal, ordinary, everyday routine, when Jesus came along and called to them. He invited them to come with him, to leave what they were doing, to leave the people they knew and loved, and to embark on a new endeavor. They answered that call. They left what they had always done, and went with him.

Now I doubt very seriously that this was the first time they had ever encountered the man Jesus. We read earlier in the Bible passage that Jesus had begun his teaching and preaching in the area, and they may well have heard him during one of those sessions. It's also possible that they had been a part of the group that was hanging around John the Baptist, and they may have encountered Jesus there. The interesting thing to me is that when Jesus called to them, they were ready and willing to answer the call. They answered with a resounding, "Yes!"

That causes me to consider what we would have done in similar circumstances. Just suppose that you and I were at the office or in the store, minding our own business, and doing what we did every single day. Just imagine that someone we've heard speak, someone we know a little about, and someone we even find a bit intriguing, comes into the place where we're working, and makes us an offer. The person extends the invitation to come and work with this new endeavor. What would you do? Would you drop everything, and go? Or would you be more likely to say, "Hey, I've got my pension to consider. The kids have college ahead, and the mortgage has to be paid. I'd better stay where I am"?

I believe that's the question and the challenge for each one of us to consider, because I'm convinced that God calls to us today just as much as in times gone by. I don't believe for a minute that God only called the likes of Abraham or Moses, or that Jesus only called those twelve disciples thousands of years ago, and stopped. I think God is calling you and me today and wants us to get a sense of who we're called to be. I honestly believe that a lot of the confusion we feel would resolve itself if we could hear and respond to God's call to us, so how do we do that? How does God call you and me? How do we begin to respond to that call?

We can encounter God in a whole variety of ways. Sometimes, for example, we experience God's call through our passions and interests. God calls us by way of the things that fascinate and interest us. What is that for you? What is it that captivates you and gets your attention? I think it's important to pay attention to whatever that is, for within it may lie God's call for us.

I also believe we can receive God's call through some of the very ordinary experiences of our everyday life, just as those fishermen along the Sea of Galilee did. We need to be alert enough to look for what's around us, and see the opportunities. In fact, I've come to believe there really is no such thing as "coincidence." Rather, it's when events and experiences converge that we can often encounter God. It's what a friend of mine refers to as a "God-cidence."

That was the way it was for me. My first awareness of a call from God came through a convergence of experiences — the deaths of two close friends in my neighborhood, being part of a women's singing group, and serving as a career development trainer for a volunteer organization in Indianapolis. Those things didn't seem like they could be at all connected, but everything came together, and I realized I was experiencing God's calling me and pointing me in a whole new direction.

What is it for you? What's happening in your life right now? What has been going on? What little seed has been planted in you that you might want to notice and be aware of? Where might God be in the midst of all of it? I think it's important to be aware of what's going on around us in the normal, everyday flow of things. You never know which experience may be God's call to us.

There's another way in which God's call can be clear to us, and that's through other people. There are people in all our lives who encourage us and affirm us — people who recognize gifts and abilities that we can't see for ourselves. There are people who challenge us to move into new territory and try new things. We need other people to help us grow, and we can help them grow, too.

We all need someone around us who really represents God. There was a person like that for me, a clergy friend who nudged and nurtured me along until I finally tiptoed my way into seminary, not entirely sure why I was there, but a seminary student nonetheless.

Who is it for you? Who is the person who encourages you to dream dreams? Who helps you be more than you ever thought you could be? All of us might want to pay close attention to who that is, because that person just might be God's calling to us.

One thing is for sure, God does call us, and that call evokes an answer from us. We have the option of saying, "No," and turning the other way, and I suspect we do that sometimes. We can back-peddle and beg off and make excuses by saying, "This isn't the right time." "We can't afford it." "I don't have the right education; I'm too young; I'm too old; I'm not smart enough." It doesn't matter what it is, we can always find a reason not to respond to God.

However, I don't think that's what God wants for us. Rather, God's call is really an invitation to embark on a journey of self-discovery. To know God's call is to begin to know ourselves, to know who we are at the center of our being. We begin to discover the interests and skills and abilities God has given us, and the gifts and passions God calls forth from us. It is in knowing ourselves that we come to know the God within us, and God's call on our lives.

It doesn't stop with knowing who we are. It means *being* that person, being who God created us to be, our very best selves, being true to ourselves, and using the gifts and talents God has given us. That's really God's call to us — to know who we're created to be, and to be the spiritual being God has designed us to be. God calls us to be ourselves, fully and completely the self we were created to be. All of life is the journey to discover who we are.

It's a great journey, but it means a little risk. Responding to and following God's call in our lives is certainly not always the easiest route to take. In fact, sometimes it seems like the most difficult. Sometimes we have to stretch to reach to new heights; we have to overcome or cope with some of our very real limitations and inadequacies. Just because we're going in the direction and headed where we believe God wants us to go doesn't mean the path will be without bumps. There will be just as many, if not more, detours and bumps along this path as along any other. However, even with all the risks, it's worth it.

Leslie Weatherhead has long been one of my favorite writers, and I really like what he says about his own call to the ministry in his classic book, *The Christian Agnostic*. After a lot of struggle and turmoil, he wrote: "I was right to want to be a minister. I had wanted to be a doctor and the conflict had been intense, but in that hour I knew the ministry was the right path for me. For me it was right, right, right ... An indescribable joy possessed me...."[1]

It probably sounds as though I'm trying to convince you to go into the ministry, and that's not the point. I am saying that it's important for each of us to discover who we are and who God is calling us to be. That's the way it was with a woman who answered the call to help other women who were trapped in a pattern of spousal abuse and domestic violence as she once had been. That's the way it was with a researcher who has devoted his life to finding a cure for a disease that took the life of a family member. That's the way it can be for each of us when we're willing to answer the call. We'll know when it's right, because everything is in synch; it all works together.

The time is now for us to follow God's call — not next week, or next month, or next year. Just step out, and give it a try. I'm convinced that we'll find God right there alongside, cheering us on, holding our hand, encouraging us, beckoning us onward.

Are you ready to answer the call?

Closing Word

When I think about God's call to us to be who we're meant to be, I get the image of a little seed, which God has planted. It's a flower seed, and soon the flower pops out of the ground, and starts to grow. First it buds, then blossoms, and then comes into full bloom. There are various types of flowers, and they're all different colors and sizes and shapes. No two are exactly alike.

Some grow best in the shade, and others need full sun. Some grow better if planted a few inches from one another, and others grow best if planted in clumps. But one thing is for sure — they're all beautiful flowers, and they are beautiful because God made them that way. They spend their entire life, no matter how brief, being what they were created to be — beautiful flowers.

That's the way it is with us humans. We are all created by God as unique, beautiful, wonderful creations. Our journey through life is one of discovering who we are, and living as that God-made spiritual being.

As you leave here this morning, I hope and pray that you're ready to answer God's call, and to become who God created you to be. Go in peace. Amen.

---

1. Leslie D. Weatherhead, *The Christian Agnostic* (Nashville: Abington Press, 1965), p. 76.

Are You Happy?

When I'm teaching a class, and want to get a discussion going, I often begin with something that's called a sentence stem. I start a sentence and let the participants complete it. This morning, if I were to ask you to complete this sentence, what would you say? "Happy are those who...." What would you use to complete the thought?

Happy are those who have lots of money and can go anywhere, do anything, have anything they want? Happy are those who are successful and well acclaimed in their businesses or professions? Happy are those who are healthy, or those who have good marriages, or who have perfect children?

I've had people sit in my office and say to me, "If only I could find the right mate, then I'd be happy." Or I've heard infertile couples say, "If we could just get pregnant and have a baby, then our happiness would be complete! Things would be perfect!" When I hear things like that, I want to shout, "No! That's not true! You're missing the point!" Happiness isn't "out there" somewhere. It's in here. If we aren't happy without a child, we won't be happy with one. If we aren't happy as we are right now, then a mate — no matter how well matched we might be — will not make us happy.

Happiness is, in John Powell's words, "an inside job."[1] If we stop to think about it, we are all smart enough to know that happiness does not come as a result of money or material possessions or from any external source. Sometimes we let ourselves believe that having all the outward looks of happiness actually means we're happy. However, happiness doesn't have anything to do with external circumstances.

In the movie, *Cool Runnings*, John Candy played a former American gold medallist who became coach to the Jamaican bobsled team. As the story evolves, the coach's dark history comes out. After his gold medal performance, his competitors discover that he broke the rules by weighting the U.S. sled. By doing so, he brought disgrace to himself and to his team. One of the Jamaican bobsledders didn't understand why someone who'd already won a medal would cheat, so he asked Candy to explain. The coach said, "I had to win, but I learned something. If you are not happy without a gold medal, you won't be happy with it."[2]

In some ways, that's what Jesus is trying to say in this familiar passage that we call the Beatitudes. If we were to take these sayings literally, we would get the wrong idea. The point Jesus is trying to make is that happiness is not found where the conventional wisdom of the world would have us believe. In essence, Jesus turns things upside down, and offers the reverse of what we might expect. Happiness is found in some unlikely places, and is a byproduct of our manner of living and our attitudes toward life.

Part of the assumption here is that God wants us to be happy. That's God's intent for our lives. Jesus knew that unhappy people tend to be self-focused, and look on the gloomy side of things. Happy people, on the other hand, have different characteristics, and tend to be more energetic, decisive, flexible, and creative. They tolerate more frustration, are more forgiving, and tend to be more willing to help those in need. At least, that's how many psychologists describe them.

What would it mean for you if you heard God say, "I want you to be happy for the rest of your life"? Given the fact that we live in a time where things are more concise and to the point, where we work in smaller sound bytes, I think Jesus would probably have distilled these thoughts on happiness down to just a few broader categories. Now I don't presume to have the mind of Jesus, but I think the new revised, updated, current version of the Beatitudes might contain just four basic premises.

First, I think Jesus would say, "Happy are those who have a good sense of self." By that, I mean accepting ourselves as we are, without having to do or be anything. We don't define our self-worth by how much money we earn, or by our achievements, or by material well-being, or by whether or not others approve. To have a good sense of self, we need only accept that we are ultimately and unconditionally accepted and loved by God.

As hard as that concept is for us to understand, I believe it is at the very core of our ability to have a good sense of who we are. It doesn't have anything to do with how we compare ourselves with others, nor does it have anything to do with the fact that we're far from perfect people. We have to give up pretending to be something we're not, and accept ourselves as we are, limitations and all. I suspect that the reason many of us are unhappy is that we're trying to be something we're not, or we're trying to do something that just isn't who we are. Living as an imperfect being is a reality. We have limitations and weaknesses, but that's all right. God loves us still, and can and does work in and through us. So, my condensed Beatitude number one would be, "Happy are those who have a good sense of self."

Secondly, Jesus would likely say, "Happy are those who have good, supportive relationships with others." True happiness comes from how we relate to and treat others. That means developing a sense of empathy for what it would be like to be inside someone else's skin. It means caring for one another, and forgiving one another's faults.

Now that's difficult enough today. There was an article in the paper about the fact that we don't cut anyone any slack these days. The writer of the article shared an experience he'd had where he was unfamiliar with an intersection, and had done the wrong thing, and as a result, had irritated several other drivers. People shouted at him angrily, and some sent certain gestures his way, while others impatiently honked their horns. Even something as simple as that everyday experience tests us in terms of how we treat one another. Jesus says that cutting one another some slack makes for happiness.

While it's impossible to be inside someone else's skin and live their experiences and understand all their feelings, it is important at least to make the effort. It is important to stop and think before we speak. Is what we're about to say loving and sensitive to the other person's perspective, or is it more reflective of our own needs and agenda?

In my other life, I was a school teacher, and I often saw some young people making fun of others, sometimes being downright cruel to a fellow student. Early in my teaching career, I observed how another teacher handled a rather sensitive situation. There was a child in her class who, like many seventh graders, was a bit "overgrown," and quite awkward. Children at that age go through growth spurts and often become awkward and uncoordinated.

As I was watching one day, my mentor-teacher said to the gangly youth, "Will you please open the window for me? It's really warm in our classroom, and I can't reach the upper windows." After the young man had done so, the teacher said to the entire class, "I just don't know what I would do without him! He's the only one who's tall enough to reach up and open the window for me." That teacher taught me a lot by her sensitivity to that student's need. She had empathy for him, and that's a piece of what it means to have supportive relationships with others.

Supportive relationships also have to do with forgiveness. We cannot be happy if we hold a grudge or harbor bitterness toward another. The greatest gift of love is forgiveness, and it may be the hardest gift for us to give. Let me ask you: "Are you holding something against someone else? A friend? Your partner? Your parents? Your employer?" Let go of it! Jesus taught us to pray, "Forgive us our trespasses as we forgive those who trespass against us." We will never be truly happy unless we can learn to forgive one another, and that's a big part of having supportive relationships with others.

A third thing I think Jesus would say today is, "Happy are those who look for good and work for good." Unhappy people tend to dwell on the down side of things, rehashing all the gory details of tragedy or heartache, while people who are happier tend to look on the good side.

70

It's hard to be what someone has called a "goodfinder." Not long ago, we had just returned from a trip, and hadn't been watching much television. As I was unpacking, I turned on the 11 o'clock news to catch up on what was going on locally, and the first three stories were real "downers." They included the fatal shooting of a state trooper, a police chase that ended in the death of a motorcyclist, and a shooting in another section of the city which had left one person seriously wounded. It may be naive, but sometimes I think we need to take a break from all the bad news that seems to surround us, because it's easy to get overwhelmed by all the agony to the point of thinking that's all there is. I think "goodfinders" are people who try to seek the good in other people, in themselves, and in every situation of life.

There's one more thing about those who look for good, and that is that they are the ones who want to work for good, too. Someone has said that the most significant thing about any task is the spirit in which it is done. Goodfinders work in a good-spirited fashion. I think that means working for the good in all things, and actively working for the well-being of all persons, and of all creation. It means our motives are oriented toward a good that's greater than our own personal gain.

Maybe the Hebrew word "shalom" says it best. "Shalom" means peace, but it really implies more than that. It is a wish for the presence of all good things and the enjoyment of all good things. It is everything that makes for the highest good for all. So the third thing Jesus would say today is, "Happy are those who look for good, and work for good."

There's one more thing I think Jesus would offer us in the concise, current version of the Beatitudes. I believe he would say, "Happy are those who have a growing faith in God." We like to think that we've got it all together, that we're in control, that we are totally self-sufficient, but that's just not so. Anyone who has heard a doctor's prognosis offering no hope, or anyone who has stood by the casket of a loved one knows that there are things far beyond our control.

Jesus would probably say that we need to face our spiritual poverty and emptiness, and recognize eventually that everyone will

71

let us down or fail to meet our emotional needs. No one can ever totally love us the way we want to be loved. Faith in God will not take away all the struggles and tragedies of life — of a spouse dying too young, of a teenager's accidental death, of a tiny baby dying of SIDS, but God's presence and love can and will comfort and sustain us, stabilize and guide us. We can experience the Godliness that is within each one of us.

There you have it — my concise, revised version of the Beatitudes. "Happy are those who have a good sense of self." "Happy are those who have good relationships with others." "Happy are those who look for good and work for good." "Happy are those who have a growing faith in God."

Now let me ask you: "Are you happy?"

Closing Word

As you leave here this morning, I pray that you allow yourself to experience all that life brings you, and in the midst of it, to know God's presence and love, for that is true happiness. Go in peace. Amen.

---

1. John Powell, S. J., *Happiness Is An Inside Job* (Allen, Texas: Tabor Publishing, 1989), p. 2.

2. *Cool Runnings*, produced by Disney, 1993.

Let Your Light Shine

I heard a story some years ago about some neighborhood children who were playing in the front yard when a fire truck zoomed past. Sitting on the front seat beside the driver was a beautiful Dalmatian, with its black and white spots. The children saw the dog, and immediately they started trying to figure out why the dog was there. What was the dog's role with the firefighters?

One five-year-old said, "I know. They use him to keep the crowds back when they go to a fire." "No," another one said, "he's there for good luck." The third child, a boy of about six-years-old, was very definite about his answer. He said, "I know why he's there. They use him to find the fire hydrant!"

In trying to figure out why the dog was there, those children were dancing close to one of the key questions with which we human beings seem to struggle: "Why are we here? What is the purpose of life?" Even more than that, "What is the purpose of *my* life? What am I supposed to be about?"

Sometimes that question is brought close to home when a friend or a colleague, someone who's a contemporary, dies unexpectedly. That seems to bring our own mortality into question, and this whole issue of purpose seems to bubble up right alongside it.

Have you ever had something like that happen? A friend, a coworker, is there one day, working right alongside you, and the next day, that person is gone. It's an eerie feeling to observe how the world just seems to go on, as though the person never existed. It makes us realize that the same thing could happen to me, and maybe, a few days later, I'll be forgotten as if I've never lived. It makes us wonder if our lives shouldn't be more than that.

That's a key question with which to wrestle. At some point in life we begin to struggle with why we are here. We often come to the realization that the trappings of stability and success are fleeting, and we begin to look for something more, something deeper, something more lasting than the run-of-the-mill life and the temporary fun of party after party.

When we realize how empty and meaningless our lives are, we begin to yearn for something more. Bob Buford, in his book, *Halftime*, calls that yearning the desire to move from success to significance.[1]

When we want to make that move, when we go from success toward significance, we start questioning life. We begin to ask questions like, "Shouldn't a person's life count for more than that?" "What is my life supposed to be?" "Aren't we supposed to count for something?"

One thing I love about the Bible is that it has such eternal, universal application. In our Bible passage for today, Jesus seems to know that we wrestle with this issue of why we are here. Once again, he demonstrates his understanding of life and human nature. Now the passage we have for today is a part of what we call the Sermon on the Mount, and, in it, Jesus is trying to help us understand just why we are here.

To define how he understands our purpose in life, he uses three analogies. In our version of scripture, Jesus says we're here to be salt-seasoning, light, and light-bearers. Let's think about those three things for a few minutes.

First, Jesus said, "You're here to be salt-seasoning," or as some other versions put it, "You are the salt of the earth." Salt is a very common, ordinary ingredient. We can find it on virtually every table, and in every kitchen cabinet. When we buy it in the grocery, it's quite inexpensive.

However, salt has an important role. I know some of us don't use it for health reasons, and probably most of us shouldn't use as much as we do, but salt makes an important contribution when it comes to eating. Why do we put salt on our food? We usually use it to enhance the flavor of what we're eating. Salt is a seasoning that adds a little zest to food, and it also enhances the flavor of the other ingredients. As our Bible passage puts it, it "brings out the God-flavors."

What would that mean if we applied it to human beings? What would it mean to think that part of our purpose in life is to be "salt-seasoning," "the salt of the earth"?

If salt adds a little zest and brings out the flavors of other things, then maybe that's what we're supposed to do in the human realm. Maybe we're here to spice up life, and help others by bringing out their particular flavors — their uniqueness, their gifts and talents, and to help them simmer to perfection.

It seems to me that one of the ways in which we can do that is by encouraging and nurturing other people. We can offer positive reinforcement and feedback. We can help others discover their gifts, and enhance their lives by helping them grow.

It's like an experience someone named Scott Adams had. One day about ten years ago, he was flipping through the channels, and saw the closing credits for a PBS broadcast called *Funny Business*, a show about cartooning. He had always wanted to be a cartoonist, but had never known how to go about it.

The host of the show was a cartoonist named Jack Cassady, and Scott Adams decided to write him a letter. He explained his interest in getting into the profession, and sent along some samples of his work. A few weeks later, he received an encouraging handwritten letter from Jack, who answered all of his specific questions about materials and process.

However, Jack did more than that. He encouraged Scott to send his work to publishers, and he went on to warn him that he would likely be rejected at first, but not to get discouraged. Jack said that his work was good, and worthy of publication. Adams got really excited, and submitted some of his best cartoons to *Playboy* and *The New Yorker*. His work was very quickly rejected, so he put all his materials away, and decided to forget about this far-fetched dream of becoming a cartoonist.

Something happened a year and a half later to change all that. Out of the blue, he received a second letter from Jack Cassady.

Cassady had been reviewing his mail files, and had run across Scott's letter. Cassady wrote this: "The reason I'm dropping you this note is to again encourage you to submit your ideas to various publications ... Sometimes encouragement in the funny business of graphic humor is hard to come by. That's why I am encouraging you to hang in there and keep drawing."

Scott Adams was very touched by Jack Cassady's letter, and acted on his encouragement. He got his art supplies back out; he drew some sample strips, and sent them off to publishers. His cartoon strip *Dilbert* now appears in 700 newspapers across the country, and he has completed six books — all because a man named Jack Cassady took the time to encourage him.[2] Jack Cassady was salt-seasoning for Scott Adams. Jesus says that's a part of our purpose on earth, to be salt-seasoning, and to help others by enhancing their lives and encouraging them as they move through life's journey.

Secondly, Jesus says we're here to be light, "bringing out the God-colors of the world." Light is an important thing, too. Think back to the story of creation. Remember that, in the beginning, everything was total darkness, and the first thing God said was, "Let there be light."

Light is important because it pierces the darkness, and brightens the grayness around us. It attracts and warms us. I always notice the difference when I'm pulling up to our house, and there are no lights on inside or out. It appears cold, bleak, uninviting. It feels much more welcoming, even if I know no one is home, to pull into the driveway and see a light on in the front hall, or upstairs. A light is inviting, and signals warmth.

Light is important because it allows us to see where we're going. That's why we turn on a light when we go into a room. We want to see where we're going. For those of us who have no night vision, it's absolutely essential in order to keep from killing ourselves in the dark.

Think what it would be like if we had no light, if there were only darkness. Think of what we would not be able to see. We couldn't see the color of our lover's eyes; we couldn't see the red-birds at our feeder. We wouldn't see the difference between the rich green hues of the summer leaves and the bright oranges and reds and golds of the fall colors. Light brings out the colors, and transforms the darkness.

So, what does it mean if we are light? It means we are to be a bright spot in life, transforming the darkness. It means that in some ways, we show the way; we illuminate the path. We're a guiding light.

But Jesus goes even farther to help us define our purpose in life. Jesus says we are to be "light-bearers," people who carry the light, and carry it so it can be seen.

The closest we can get to understanding that is to think back to 1996 when people were carrying the Olympic torch to Atlanta for the summer games. Did you see it when it went through our town? I wasn't able to, but I talked with someone who had actually carried the torch a short distance. She said it was the most phenomenal experience of her life, and it was truly amazing because she felt that the small flame she carried was lighting up both her life and everyone's hearts.

If that's how some people felt carrying the Olympic torch, can you imagine what it might feel like to be a light-bearer the way Jesus is talking about it? How might it feel if we understood that our purpose in life is to be a light-bearer for God, and to be one carrying the light of God for others to see? The light of God is seen by how we live our lives, how we relate to others, how we treat our fellow human beings. In some way, we are to be an example for others, and a guiding light for others to follow.

To be a guiding light, a light-bearer, is an awesome responsibility! It's also a significant reason for being, to be one of God's light-bearers, reflecting the light and love of God in everything we do, and in everything we are.

I got home late from a meeting one night, and received a call telling me that a long-time friend had died. She was someone I'd call a light-bearer, someone who's had an impact on my life. She was in her early sixties, and I've probably known her ten years or so. She had spent a lot of her time visiting those in nursing homes or those who were homebound. She could literally brighten a room by her presence, and her smile always lit up everything. She would always greet me with a hug, and I knew for sure that she loved me. She was a light in my life.

I also think of a woman who was in her late eighties when she died recently. She was a frail, petite woman, who was a light in my life, too, but the irony is that she was almost totally blind, and probably couldn't see much of the light. She would come out of church, come up to me, throw her arms around me, and say, "How ya' doin', honey?" She always had a smile ready, and she was a great encourager, always being the first to compliment, the first to applaud. She was a true light-bearer.

Both of those women have been important light-bearers in my life. Do you know someone like them, someone whom you'd call a light-bearer? Do you think anyone would see God's light shining through us? Would someone call you or me a light-bearer?

Closing Word

Someone told about a friend who was caught in an elevator in New York City during a power failure. He was caught along with several other people, all strangers to one another. They were riding up in the elevator, shoulder to shoulder, not speaking, when suddenly the elevator jerked to a stop, and everything went dark. The friend said fear and panic were evident. Everyone talked at once, and then they all got quiet.

Fortunately, the friend remembered that he had something to help. He had a tiny flashlight with him, one he always carried in his pocket for situations like this. He got it out and turned it on, and everything changed. That little bit of light totally transformed the situation! The fear faded, and the trapped comrades began to tell jokes, and laugh. They even sang some songs. By the time they were rescued 45 minutes later, they had become friends. That was all because of the light that pierced their darkness, and changed everything.

As you leave here this morning, remember that Jesus said we're here to be salt-seasoning. We're here to be light, and we're here to be light-bearers.

Carry the light of God into your homes and schools, into your place of work; carry it into every corner of the world. Be the light of God, and let it shine through you. And go in peace. Amen.

78

1. Bob Buford, *Halftime* (Grand Rapids, Michigan: Zondervan Publishing House, 1994), pp. 83-84.

2. *Chicken Soup For The Soul At Work: 101 Stories Of Courage, Compassion And Creativity In The Workplace* (Chicken Soup for the Soul Series), by Jack Canfield, editor, et al., November 1996. Used by permission.

Building Bridges

There was a story on CNN a few months ago about a town in Wales that was divided by a river. For centuries, residents had gone from one part of the town across to the other by way of a ferry. Now the town was in an uproar because there was a movement afoot to build a bridge that would connect the two parts of the town. Some of the people were concerned because the bridge would put the ferry owner out of business. Others were upset because the bridge would do away with the traditional way of getting from one side to the other. Most of those who were opposed to the bridge finally admitted that they were against it because they really didn't want to be that closely connected with the people on the other side. They liked the distance between them as it was.

Having grown up on the banks of the Ohio River in Madison, I can understand a bit of what was going on in that town in Wales. When I was a child, my parents and I used to go to visit my uncle, who lived upriver from us in Warsaw, Kentucky. There were two ways we could do that. We could drive up the Indiana side a short distance, and take the little one-car ferry across to Ghent, and then drive the few miles to his home. I never liked it when my parents decided to go that way. Even though the river was less than a mile wide there, the ferry seemed to take forever! It made it seem like a very long way from the Indiana to the Kentucky side of the river.

Now the other way we could cross over to Kentucky was to go across the bridge at Madison that connected it to Milton, Kentucky. Again, the bridge was only a mile or so in length, but that trip took only about sixty seconds. The bridge brought the two

81

sides much closer together. It did what bridges are supposed to do — bring things that are separated closer together.

When we see a bridge, we can assume that there are distances, separations, or gaps that need to be narrowed. Obviously, this isn't always just over a body of water. All we have to do is to look around us, and we can see that there are plenty of gaps that need to be bridged — gaps in our relationships with one another. Distances can occur between us in even our very closest relationships — with our best friend, with our co-workers, even in our own homes. Instead of being close and intimate, our most cherished relationships often wind up feeling very distant and remote. Rifts can happen between life partners or in families. I've known families where mothers and daughters, sons and fathers, brothers, sisters, aunts and uncles, have refused to speak to one another or be in the same place at the same time, and this has gone on for years!

A similar thing can happen in our work world, when co-workers are in competition with one another, each one looking for the promotion or the raise or recognition. They would never consider turning to the person in the next cubicle with a question or a helpful hint. I wonder if that isn't why there is so much resistance to creating teamwork in the workforce. Team building tears down the old hierarchical structures that arbitrarily created distance between us. In the old days, workers knew their places and their roles and all the rules, but working as a team changes all that. It puts everyone on the same level, and that can be very threatening.

Whatever the reason, I suspect we'd all agree that there are plenty of places in each of our lives where we are distanced from one another. There are ruptures and gaps that keep us apart, which is precisely what our Bible passage for today is all about. It is saying that if there is something between us and another person — anger, a rift, alienation, bad feelings, then we've got a problem. Being distanced from other people creates distance in our relationship with God. The two are very closely intertwined.

It's like a well-known story about Leonardo da Vinci. When he was painting *The Last Supper*, he got involved in a terrible argument with a fellow artist. He was just at the point of painting the disciples around the table, and he was so angry with the man

82

that he decided to paint his fellow artist's face as the face of Judas, the one who betrayed Jesus. When he had finished, everyone could see that he had done just that! The painter's face was easily recognized.

However, there was a problem for da Vinci, because next it was time to paint the face of Jesus. He wasn't able to do it. Something was blocking every effort. Finally, after a lot of soul searching, he realized that the cause of his problem was his bitterness and lack of forgiveness toward this fellow painter. It was only after he came to terms with that, and moved toward reconciliation in the relationship that he was able to paint the face of Jesus. He was separated from God because he was separated from another person.[1]

In our Bible passage, Jesus is saying that if we are at odds with someone else, if there is a distance in any of our relationships with one another, if there is a gap between us, there is also a gap between us and God. We cannot truly expect to have a close, intimate relationship with God unless and until we do something about the distance between us as human beings. That means that the first order of business is doing our part to narrow the gap. The key to a right relationship with God comes in the course of building bridges that connect us more closely to one another.

How do we go about that? How can we begin to narrow the distance between us? The Bible passage gives us a good place to start. It says, "If you enter a place of worship ... and you suddenly remember a grudge a friend has against you...." In other words, when we connect with God, it is very probable that we will become aware of the hurtful actions, unkind words, and self-centered behaviors which have hurt our friends or loved ones. We will become more aware of how our words and deeds affect other people; we will see ourselves in a new way, in a more honest way.

In a very real way, we are attempting to see ourselves as God sees us, with all pretenses and disguises dropped. When we do that, we see ourselves for who and what we are; we see ourselves more honestly. We know that each of us is a creation of God, and loved by God, but we also come face-to-face with the ways in which we are demanding, hurtful, apathetic, and uncaring. Being more closely attuned to God allows us to experience the regret and remorse for our past actions.

Once we realize how we have contributed to the distance that exists between us, the Bible passage makes it very clear what we have to do next — *go* to the other person, and make it right. Whatever the reason, we are to take the first step. It doesn't say to sit there and wait until the other person initiates contact or comes groveling for forgiveness. It says we are to go and make it right, and then we can come back and work things out with God.

That's a tough order, and the only way to make things right and to begin building a bridge between us, is to take the first step. That means we start by loving one another, and forgiving one another. In fact, I'd go so far as to say it begins and ends with forgiveness.

An unknown author once said, "Love is an endless act of forgiveness,"[2] and I definitely believe that writer was on target. Author Henri Nouwen defined forgiveness this way: "Love practiced among people who love poorly."[3]

Forgiveness is hard, but if we really want to experience God's love fully in our lives, we have to take steps to bridge the gap between us, and that means we have to forgive. We often spend a lot of time and energy building up our defenses, making excuses for ourselves, explaining how right we were or why we did what we did. When we build those barriers of self-defense, we do more damage to our relationships, and increase the distance between us.

However, when we really realize and understand and acknowledge the role we play in wrongdoing, and when we drop our defenses, there's an amazing freeing of the burden we carry. It's as though we've punched a hole in the wall of our defense mechanisms, and we begin to leave room for God's love to fill us. When we let down the barriers of self-defense, it's then that God's love can permeate our lives in an entirely new, life-giving way. It fills us with love for one another, the kind of love that allows us to go to the person we've wronged, and, as the Bible passage says, "Make it right."

84

What does that mean, "Make it right"? It means admitting what we've done or said. It means being sorry, really sorry, for the wrongs we've committed and apologizing for them. It means saying the words, "I'm sorry. Please forgive me."

I read somewhere that the three hardest things for us to say are, "I was wrong," "I'm sorry," and "I love you." Yet, if we want to "make things right," those are words we have to practice saying. Forgiveness is the ultimate gift of love, but it's not a natural thing; it's not an easy thing. Forgiveness means we refuse to hold onto past hurts, and choose instead to release grievances and let go of blame. Forgiveness is our only hope, because it leads us to a different way of relating. It lowers the barriers between us, and, subsequently, opens wide the door for a relationship with God.

"Making it right" adds another dimension, too. It's not just the words we say. It's the action we take to move toward reconciliation and restoration of the relationship. I'm not naive, and I'm not saying that the relationship will be the same as before. I am convinced, however, that a relationship can be changed from one filled with hard feelings and animosity, to one that is filled with good will toward one another.

As a pastor, I have often visited patients who are near death, and all too often, there is someone in their lives from whom they are estranged. It might be a brother or a sister, or someone who was once a dear friend. More than once, the one dying has expressed a desire to talk with the other person to try to make things right. When that has been possible, it is amazing to see the transformation that happens! Quite often, the two see one another with different eyes, and they're able to see one another as the people they once loved and cherished. Things tend to take on a different perspective when someone is on his deathbed, and seeing through eyes of love and forgiveness can change everything. No longer is that relationship distant and remote, but a bridge of acceptance, love, forgiveness, and understanding has been built.

That's exactly what it takes to bring us closer to one another and to God. That's the only way we'll ever really be able to bridge the gaps between us.

Closing Word

To paraphrase our Bible passage for today, "If, as you came here this morning, you remembered a grudge someone has against you, leave from here today, go to that person, and make it right." Build a bridge of love, and go in peace. Amen.

---

1. Source unknown.

2. Kay Allenbaugh, *Chocolate For A Woman's Soul,* (New York, New York: Fireside, 1997), p. 145.

3. Philip Yancey, *What's So Amazing About Grace?* (Grand Rapids, Michigan: Zondervan Publishing House, 1997), p. 92.

Epiphany 7
Matthew 5:38-48

You Want Me To Do What?

There's an old Charles Schulz *Peanuts* cartoon that has Lucy chasing Charlie Brown around the house yelling, "I'll get you, Charlie Brown!" Suddenly Charlie stops, and Lucy comes to a screeching halt. Charlie says to her, "If we, who are children, cannot forgive one another, how can we expect our parents, who are adults, to forgive one another, and in turn, how can the world ..." At that point, Lucy punches Charlie Brown in the nose, knocking him down. The last frame has Lucy explaining to a friend, "I had to do it ... He was beginning to make sense."

In some ways, I feel a bit like Charlie Brown in trying to address this particular passage of scripture. Most of the time, the passages fit our sensibilities, but I'm not sure this one does that easily. Actually, it is asking an almost impossible thing from us, and that's what makes it so hard to consider. Our response to what Jesus said could well be, "You want me to do what? Love my enemy?!"

If we look more closely at the passage, and most of all at the commandment to love our enemies, perhaps we can come to some new understanding of what Jesus might have meant. Many of us wrestle with our perspectives and attitudes and with how our faith is relevant and comes to bear on this issue. In theory, loving our enemies sounds ideal, but it's hard to imagine being filled with love when we look into the face of someone who murdered a friend or family member, or some person or group or nation who has caused us pain and heartache.

I recall an experience that occurred early in my ministry, an experience that taught me just how hard it is to think about loving someone who has committed a wrongful act. Our congregation had sponsored a Vietnamese family to come to the United States, and the family consisted of two brothers, and their niece and nephew.

Just six months after they arrived in the States, as the two youngsters were walking to school early in the morning, the six-year-old boy was struck and killed by a drunk driver. I was with the uncles at the hospital as we tried to come to terms with what had happened, and a few months later, several of us from the church sat in the courtroom listening to the proceedings. We were asked to speak when it came time for the sentencing, and that was one of the most difficult things I've ever had to do!

While I personally had prayed hard about forgiving the driver for what she had done, I discovered that wasn't a simple thing. I looked into her face, knowing that she was a mother herself, knowing what her imprisonment would mean for her family, knowing the remorse she had expressed, and yet I still felt an intense dislike of her. She had not wronged me personally, and yet I was indignant about what she had done, and felt almost hatred toward her.

Frankly, that frightened me a lot, and I've prayed hard over the years to be able to forgive her, and even to begin to love her. I don't know if I'm there yet, or not, but I can testify to the personal turmoil this has caused me. Loving our enemy is a difficult undertaking. I've discovered that it's an easy thing to spout platitudes like that from the pulpit, but it's a tough thing to live them out in our everyday lives.

That's a dilemma many of us face, and, as people of faith, I think it's one with which we need to struggle, since I doubt that many of us see the matter as clearly defined. As people of faith, we have to wrestle with how to deal with our enemies and how we live out the commandment to love them.

Jesus says we are to love our enemies, but first we must determine who that is. Who is the enemy? In the Bible passage, the enemy is understood to be the non-Israelite, anyone who might be different. If each of us took a moment to stop and think about it, we might well be able to conjure up in our minds the ones we would call "enemy."

Perhaps the enemy is not someone as far away as a foreign leader or a hostile people. In a Bible study group, the participants were discussing this same passage, and the leader asked those in the group to think of the person toward whom they felt the most hostility. Suddenly, a woman in the group gasped and said, "It's my husband!" It took her by surprise that one she loved was also one she could call enemy, and that he could be so close at hand.

Who are our enemies, the ones who are the nemesis in our lives? Perhaps it's a co-worker who's irritable or power-hungry or self-aggrandizing. Maybe it's a boss who's demanding, insensitive, unreasonable, or it might be an ex-spouse whose presence fills us with hatred and bitterness. It could be a former business associate who acted unethically and caused the business to fail. Maybe it's someone who maligned us or treated us unfairly. It could be someone we find difficult to deal with, someone who brings out the worst in us, causing us to feel negative or angry. Whoever it is, one thing is for sure — Jesus mentioned enemies because he assumed we would have some. He was addressing a situation in which most of us find ourselves at one time or another.

Given that, why would Jesus, knowing how it is for us, tell us to do something like *loving* our enemy? I believe Jesus said what he did because he understood our human nature all too well, and he knew that our first tendency is to want revenge. We are filled with anger and resentment, and we want to get back at the one who hurts us.

Now granted, there are times when anger is appropriate and justified, and when it is creative and brings about change. The story of Jesus in the Temple upsetting the tables of the money-changers is often cited as an example of this. Jesus was rightly angry because the moneychangers were cheating others and taking advantage of them. He was angry at immoral actions.

Anger is often the normal human response, but the problem occurs when we hold onto our anger, and that's what Jesus understood. That's why he reminds us once again that love is the better way. It's the better way to live with ourselves and with others, and it's the better way to deal with our enemies because it ultimately results in good, and not something destructive. Jesus wants us to have lives of wholeness and healing, and he promotes positive relationships to further that end.

Even knowing all that, how can we ever begin to love our enemies? Are there limits to what we take from others? How are we to love?

The kind of love discussed in the Bible passage is an "agape" kind of love, the kind of love God has for us. It is a love that implies involvement, concern, caring, and sacrifice. It is unconditional, supportive, and firm. It is the kind of love that calls forth profound changes from within us, and radical changes in the way we live and relate to one another.

Perhaps it is akin to the kind of love a parent has for a child. As parents, we care about our children and their well-being. Consequently, we try to raise them lovingly, but that love is not permissive love. We don't condone every action, and we teach our children the repercussions of their acts. We don't allow them to touch a hot stove because they might get burned. We teach them to be responsible drivers so they won't harm themselves or others. I've always told our daughter that hitting someone is an inappropriate way to resolve differences, and I've tried to teach her to live within parameters. Love does not mean that anything goes.

How do we begin the difficult task of trying to love our enemies, something that flies in the face of our human nature? The first thing we have to do is to decide to be more loving. It must be an intentional act because that's exactly what love is — action. When a drunk driver has caused our bodies to become permanently disabled, and forever altered our lives, we have to make a clear and conscious decision that we're going to love the person who hurt us. Otherwise, we will be destroyed in more than our bodies. Our spirits will be forever imprisoned by the bitterness and hatred.

It isn't easy, and it isn't something that happens overnight. However, we have to decide we want to be loving and forgiving to our enemies; then perhaps we can begin to understand them. If we had been born into the same set of circumstances and exposed to the same kind of influences, maybe we, too, would have acted in the same way. We have to begin to put a human face on our enemies if we are to love them, and we have to see them as fellow human beings who are hurting as we are.

As people of faith, we must wrestle with this tough issue, and we must begin today. Our fervent prayer must be for God's love to permeate our hearts and lessen the hardness we feel toward others. We need to pray to be able to love those we call our enemies.

I heard a story a long time ago about the life-changing power of that agape kind of love. A company of soldiers had traveled from Malta to Egypt, and everyone was ready to turn in for the night. They were all wet and muddy from the rain, and thoroughly exhausted.

One young private quietly knelt beside his bed to pray, but his sergeant took offense to this display of faith, and reached for one of his boots. He hit the private on the side of his head with that rain-soaked boot, and then he took the other boot and hit him on the other side of his face.

The soldier's face stung from the pain, as well as from the humiliation, and after the sergeant went to sleep, the soldier paid him back. When the sergeant awoke the next morning, he found his boots beautifully polished and standing neatly beside his bed. As that crusty sergeant told this story later, he said that the private's reply to him had broken his heart. He confessed that he had run up against the power of love, and he had been different ever since.

That's what the power of God's love can do, and that's why we must pray for God's loving touch to soften our hearts. Jesus' admonition to love our enemies is a tough one, but that's exactly what he wants us to do, and we need to begin right this moment.

Closing Word

As we leave here this morning, I hope and pray that you and I are willing to let go of the love of power in favor of the power of love. Have a good Sunday, and go in peace. Amen.

Why Worry?

We were told that one of the major trends of the latter part of the twentieth century was anxiety. Many people were worried about the new millennium, and there were concerns about Y2K, and how it would affect our lives. It was hard to find a newscast that didn't make at least some mention of it, and there were numerous interviews with people who had stocked up supplies of food and water, batteries and blankets. Some had even stored guns because they believed a state of anarchy would reign!

I saw a show where the reporter was interviewing someone in the government who was responsible for seeing that all governmental agencies were Y2K compliant. She said they weren't in very good shape. As a matter of fact, she stated that it was so bad that — heaven forbid! — they might have to go back to using paper and pencil to do their work! There was a chance that some offices would even have to shut down because of the Y2K thing! That might not have been all bad!

Perhaps it was not Y2K that you and I worried about, but I'd be willing to bet that most of us have worried about someone or something within the last 24 hours! That just seems to be a normal human thing. Our daughter recently had to spend a few days doing something brand new for her job. Fortunately, she only found out about it the day before, but she did her fair share of worrying before the job began.

I was chatting with a friend whose significant other is an airline pilot. There had been an airline crash the day before, and she had a very concerned look on her face. Immediately, she started talking about how worried she was when her pilot friend was flying, and this mishap only served to compound her worry. How many of us have done something like that — worried ourselves sick about someone we love?

The truth is that most of us worry about all kinds of things — from the profound to the mundane. Along with worrying about the safety and well-being of those we love, we worry about things like walking into a room of strangers, looking foolish, or seeming stupid when we ask a question. Sometimes we're worried about what people think of us, but Olin Miller was correct when he said, "We probably wouldn't worry about what people think of us if we could know how seldom they do."[1] That's certainly some food for thought.

Let's stop to think a minute about what worry actually is. It's significant that it comes from an Anglo-Saxon word that means "to strangle" or "to choke."[2] That means that worry can actually get a strangle hold on us, and literally cut off the air supply that allows us to breathe! Worry, anxiety, concern and apprehension — all synonyms — really keep us from living our lives to the very fullest because we are always filled with fear that something awful is about to happen. Arthur Somers Roche once said, "Worry is a thin stream of fear trickling through the mind. If encouraged, it cuts a channel into which all other thoughts are drained."[3]

The bottom line is that worry is not a very beneficial activity, and there are several reasons to say that. For one thing, worry can actually be damaging to our health. Dr. Charles Mayo says, "Worry affects the circulation, the heart, the glands, the whole nervous system."[4] Worry can totally consume us, and if it doesn't cause us to die physically, it can certainly keep us from enjoying life on a daily basis.

Worry can lead to some rather unsavory results. Apparently, movie actor David Niven was a terrible worrier and that was manifested by his habitual nail-biting. As the story goes, Niven received a postcard one day from his friend, Noel Coward, who was traveling in Italy. The card showed a picture of the famous *Venus de Milo* and said, "You see what will happen if you keep biting your nails?"[5] That's just one of the unpleasant consequences of constant worrying.

There's more. Worry really wastes a lot of time and energy. Do you realize how few of the things we worry about actually happen? A recent survey says that forty percent of the things we worry about never happen, and another thirty percent of our worries are in the past, and we can't do anything about them. Twelve percent of our worries concern other people, and are really none of our business anyway. Another ten percent are about sickness, which we can do very little to control. Only eight percent of the things we worry about are said to be worth worrying about.[6] Worry is really a useless activity.

So, what do we do with all our worries? That's where the Bible passage for today comes in. This is part of the wisdom Jesus shared with us in the Sermon on the Mount. It tells us not to worry about things like clothes or food or drink. Those are not the most important things in life, and we can trust God to take care of us and give us whatever we need to survive. As a friend of mine likes to say, "God will provide."

So many of the things you and I worry about really don't matter much in the whole scheme of things. Maybe the next time we catch ourselves worrying about something, we should stop and ask ourselves, "Is this really going to matter five years from now? Or even next week?" Often I suspect our answer will be "No." No one will know or care about the issue that seems so critical to us at this very moment. We just need to learn to weigh things a little differently when it comes to our worries, and sort things out. Then we need to let go, and put our trust in God who does truly provide, and even in some wonderful, surprising ways.

Let me suggest a couple of things that we might do to begin to let go of our worries. First we might start trying to remedy the situation rather than just fretting about it. Astronaut Jim Lovell was in command of the Apollo 13 spacecraft when it experienced an explosion on its way to the moon. Their oxygen was almost gone; their electrical system was out, and their spaceship was plunging toward lunar orbit. It looked as if they were destined to be lost in space, thousands of miles from home.

During a press conference after their safe return, Lovell was asked, "Were you worried?" and he gave an answer that surprised almost everyone in the room. "No, not really." He continued, "Worry is a useless emotion. I was too busy fixing the problem to worry about it."[7] Maybe we would be better served by putting our energies into finding a solution to the problem rather than just worrying about it.

There's another thing, too, that can help us let go of some of our worries. I heard about a guy who handled his worries in a creative fashion. Because there seemed to be so many things to worry about, he decided to set aside one day each week in which to worry. So, as worries came to him, he would write them down and put them in his worry box. Then, on the day he had chosen, Worry Wednesday, he pulled out each worry and read it. He discovered that most of the things he was disturbed about had already settled themselves or been taken care of in some other way. He learned that there was seldom a real reason to worry, and he began to eliminate worry from his life.[8]

Maybe you and I can try that — writing down all our worries and putting them in a file or a box, and only dealing with them one day a week. We just might come to the same discovery — that the things we're so concerned about have a way of working themselves out.

There's another thing that might work when it comes to dealing with our worries, and that's praying about them. As someone said, "If our worries aren't worth praying about, they aren't worth worrying about."[9] How true that is! It helps if we turn to God in prayer, and let go of our worries. The problem with most of us is that we pray about them, but we don't let go. We have a tendency to take them back and continue to worry.

However, if we genuinely turn our worries over to God, I believe we'll find that the process of praying about them can ease the anxiety and maybe even plant a few notions in our minds about how to address them. Prayer works, and it works because God does. It works because we can trust God to be there, to care for us, to provide for us. That's the Good News, so why worry?

Closing Word

When it comes to our worries, we have access to an anti-worry potion that never fails. It's God, who can allay our fears, calm our anxieties, and allow us to let go of our worries. So as you leave here this morning, know you can trust God, and go in peace. Amen.

---

1. Olin Miller, *Quotable Quotes* (Pleasantville, New York: Reader's Digest, 1997), p. 16.

2. Glenn Van Ekeren, *Words For All Occasions* (Paramus, New Jersey: Prentice Hall, 1988), p. 393.

3. James Hewitt, *Illustrations Unlimited* (Wheaton, Illinois: Tyndale House Publishers, Inc., 1988), p. 496.

4. Dr. Charles Mayo, "Worry," *Dynamic Illustrations*, JAS 1999.

5. David Niven, "Worry," *Dynamic Illustrations*, JAS 1999.

6. Ekeren, *op. cit.*, pp. 392-393.

7. Mort Crim, *Second Thoughts* (Deerfield Beach, Florida: Health Communications, Inc., 1997), pp. 153-154.

8. Ekeren, *op. cit.*, p. 392.

9. "Worry," *Dynamic Illustrations*, JAS 1998.

Transfiguration Of The Lord
(Last Sunday After Epiphany)
Matthew 17:1-9

It's A Mystery

Mike, a member of our Good Earth Band at THE GARDEN, and a Ph.D. chemist at Eli Lilly Company, filled in for me when I was away. He decided to use some of his chemical know-how to make the point he wanted to make. Mike had three styrofoam cups and a pitcher of water. He poured water into one of the cups, and did the moving-the-cups-around-routine, asking those who were watching to keep their eye on the cup with the water in it. After he had completed his "hocus-pocus," he asked them to tell him which cup had the water. Most folks were fairly clear on which cup it was, but when Mike turned it upside down, it was empty.

For them, it was a mystery! As it turns out, the scientist-turned-preacher had put a white, powdery substance in the cup into which he had poured the water. That white powder is the same substance that is used in babies' diapers to make them water-absorbent. It's invisible; no one could see the powder, and as if by magic, the water he had poured into the cup was absorbed and disappeared.

I tell you that story by way of saying that the Bible passage we have for today, the story that's called "The Transfiguration," is a bit of a mystery to me. In fact, when I read the commentaries and did my study on the passage, I felt totally unclear on what it was all about, and what was happening. However, as I reflected on it, it occurred to me that that might be precisely the main message in this story.

There is a part of what we experience in the spiritual realm of our lives that is quite mysterious, and difficult to explain. For example, there's a man whom I've known for years, who happened to be leaving a meeting at the church one night, heading home. When he got to the street and started to make the turn toward home, he seemed to hear a voice telling him to turn the other way. He paused, shook it off, and started to turn in the direction of his home, but as he did, he heard the voice again. This time, he decided to heed it, and he turned the other direction.

After he had driven a short distance in the wrong direction, wondering why on earth he had made that turn, he came upon a minor accident. It turned out to be a person who had been in the meeting with him and had left earlier. He was the first person on the scene, called the police, and waited with his friend until help arrived.

Now you can call that whatever you like, but I think it's a mystery. Having said that, however, I also have to admit that I believe that there is much "out there" around us that we don't know about, and don't really understand. Our eyes are not clear enough, and we aren't astute enough to perceive all that is around us.

As I think about the Bible passage for this morning, I can't tell you whether or not this was an actual God-thing, but I tend to believe that something special happened to those who were gathered on top of that mountain. For one thing, mountains have long been understood as a place that is holy, and where holy encounters can and do occur. Throughout the Bible, we find stories of those who have encountered God or had spiritual experiences on the mountain. I know that's been true for me. When I go to the mountains, I come away feeling spiritually renewed and re-centered. I feel that I can see more clearly, and I suspect that is what those in our Bible passage were experiencing.

Part of what this passage is telling us is that it's important to put ourselves in places, and open our eyes in such a way to take in the mysterious, the holy, the spiritual. Sometimes we have to pause long enough to appreciate the wonder and awe of life all around us.

In some ways, it may be a little bit like something that happened to an emergency room physician named Harry. He was on his shift one night when a woman was brought in about to give birth. As soon as he got there, he realized that, unless her obstetrician was already somewhere in the building, he was going to deliver this baby himself. Everyone scurried about, making all the preparations, and the baby was born almost immediately.

Harry laid the infant girl along his left forearm, and took a suction bulb and began to clear her mouth and nose. Suddenly, the baby opened her eyes and looked directly at him. In that moment, Harry said he stepped out of his technical role, and realized a very simple thing: He was the first human being this baby girl had ever seen. He felt his heart go out to her in welcome from all people everywhere and tears came to his eyes. Harry had delivered hundreds of babies, but he admitted that he had never allowed himself to experience the meaning of what he was doing before. In some very real way, Harry believes this is the first baby that he ever really delivered.[1] Harry experienced a moment of awe and wonder, and that made all the difference, and what he experienced was something that was invisible, intangible, yet very real.

That reminds me of that well-known line in the classic story of "The Little Prince." At the end, the fox and the little prince have become friends, but it's time for them to part. The fox then shares with him the secret of life — a very simple secret. He says, "It is only with the heart that one can see rightly; what is essential is invisible to the eye."[2] And so it is.

A mountaintop experience can certainly be a spiritual "high," and it can affect us in a variety of ways. In our Bible passage, it seemed to fire Peter up. He wanted to build three buildings, and he was "babbling" on about that possibility, when something stopped him in his tracks. I wonder if that something was a reminder that action is not always the best course. There are plenty of times in life when we need to slow down, and look and listen. We need to contemplate and consider our experiences.

There are times for stillness in life, and probably most of us could benefit by learning to experience and appreciate those times of quiet. After all, our world has a way of inundating us with information and stimuli, and life is moving at an incredible pace! With personal communications systems, paging devices, cell phones, faxes, e-mail, and voice mail, communication is instantaneous, or as close as it can get to it.

We're told that there's more information for us to assimilate than ever before. In fact, I read somewhere that we are now exposed to more information in one Sunday's newspaper than the average person was exposed to in a whole year during the 1700s! And this is only the tip of the iceberg!

How, in the midst of all that, can we possibly find ways to "Be still, and know that I am God" (Psalm 46:10)? The Bible passage for today is encouraging us to stop and slow down, to take time out and look and listen, and become aware of God in perhaps an entirely new way. How can we do that? How can we slow down our hurrying, and begin to appreciate the awe and wonder, the beauty and mystery all around us?

I want to make something clear. I believe that God is present in every moment and in every experience of life. God is in the hectic, crazy, frantic pace of life as well as in the cool ocean breeze and the quiet starlit night. God is in everything, in everyone, and is everywhere.

However, we're the problem. When we're moving a million miles an hour, we miss God. It's not that God isn't there, it's just that we're too preoccupied and too distracted, and we simply aren't aware of God's presence. We're not focused enough to experience the divine touch in our midst. That's why we need to take some time to be still; we need to be still to become aware of ourselves, and to experience God's presence within us and around us in new and different ways.

How do we do that? I have to tell you that I don't have all the answers. To be truthful, I have to admit that I've got this busy-ness part down pat; it's the quieting and being still that I haven't quite managed very well yet.

However, other people's experiences can be helpful. For instance, I heard someone once talk about envisioning ourselves as being in the eye of a storm. The eye of a storm is the one spot in the center of a hurricane that is totally calm, and almost isolated from the violence and turbulence around it. No matter how crazy it gets, the center remains quiet and still.

Perhaps what you and I need to do is develop the art of discovering that same kind of calm in the midst of the chaos of our lives.

Maybe it's through meditation, or prayer, or taking mini-vacations in our minds, or going out into nature, or sitting in a room alone in silence.

At the beginning or the end of the day, maybe we need just to pull our car over and stop. Perhaps there's a place where we can catch our breath, and take in the view; or maybe it's a matter of just closing our eyes and breathing deeply for a moment. Most of us need some time when we can slow down, and become more centered and focused. Instead of rushing to work with the radio blaring, that might be the time to be quiet and experience God.

There are other ways to "be still," and experience God, too. In her book, *When The Heart Waits,* Sue Monk Kidd tells about a lesson she learned when she was a child. It has to do with taking the time to allow ourselves to see and experience something we may never have seen before. When Sue was young, a woman named Sweet took care of her. She said that one day, the two of them started out for one of Sue's favorite places, the city park, that was about four blocks from her home. Sue was anxious to get there, but that day Sweet took her hand and headed out in the wrong direction. "We're taking the long way round," Sweet said.

That felt like a curse for a young child, because it meant at least eight blocks rather than the normal four! It was awful, but Sweet would not give in, so off they went. They had walked about six of those eight blocks when Sweet stopped beside a ditch that was swollen with water and tadpoles. She pulled out a Mason jar from her pocket, one that already had nail holes punched in the lid. Sweet looked at Sue Monk Kidd, smiled, and said, "Now aren't you glad we took the long way round? No tadpoles the short way."[3]

Sometimes for us it may be taking the long way round. It's taking time to slow down, to experience the mysteries of God all around us, to sense the wonder of God within us. It's important to acknowledge the need for a time to be still; it's planning for it; it's building it into our day. It's finding a time and a way to get re-newed and re-centered and refreshed. It's being still, and letting God's presence surround us, and God's spirit fill us.

103

Closing Word

As you leave here this morning, slow down and live; be quiet, and look for the mystery of God all around us. And go in peace. Amen.

---

1. "Sleight of Hand," "I Never Promised You A Rose Garden," "Surprised by Meaning," from *Kitchen Table Wisdom* by Rachel Naomi Remen, M.D., copyright © 1996 by Rachel Naomi Remen, M.D. Used by permission of Putnam Berkley, a division of Penguin Putnam Inc.

2. Antoine Saint-Exupery, *The Little Prince*, (New York: Harcourt, Inc., 1943), p. 63.

3. Pages 18 and 19 from *When The Heart Waits* by Sue Monk Kidd. Copyright © 1990 by Sue Monk Kidd. Reprinted by permission of HarperCollins Publishers, Inc.

SECOND LESSON SET
Holy E-Mail
Sermons For Advent/Christmas/Epiphany
Dallas A. Brauninger

Access To High Hope
Sermons For Lent/Easter
Harry N. Huxhold

Acting On The Absurd
Sermons For Sundays After Pentecost (First Third)
Gary L. Carver

A Call To Love
Sermons For Sundays After Pentecost (Middle Third)
Tom M. Garrison

Distinctively Different
Sermons For Sundays After Pentecost (Last Third)
Gary L. Carver